City of Sunderland College

Hylton Learning Workshop

This book is due for return on or before the last date shown below
Please be aware that fines are charged for overdue items
Renew online: http://heritageonline.citysun.ac.uk
Renew by phone: call 5116231

30 MAR 2012

30/8/2013

21 DAY LOAN

the *complete* guide to
massage

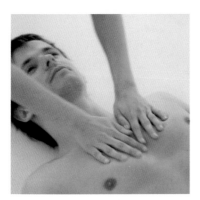

the *complete* guide to
massage
susan mumford

BB Bounty
Books

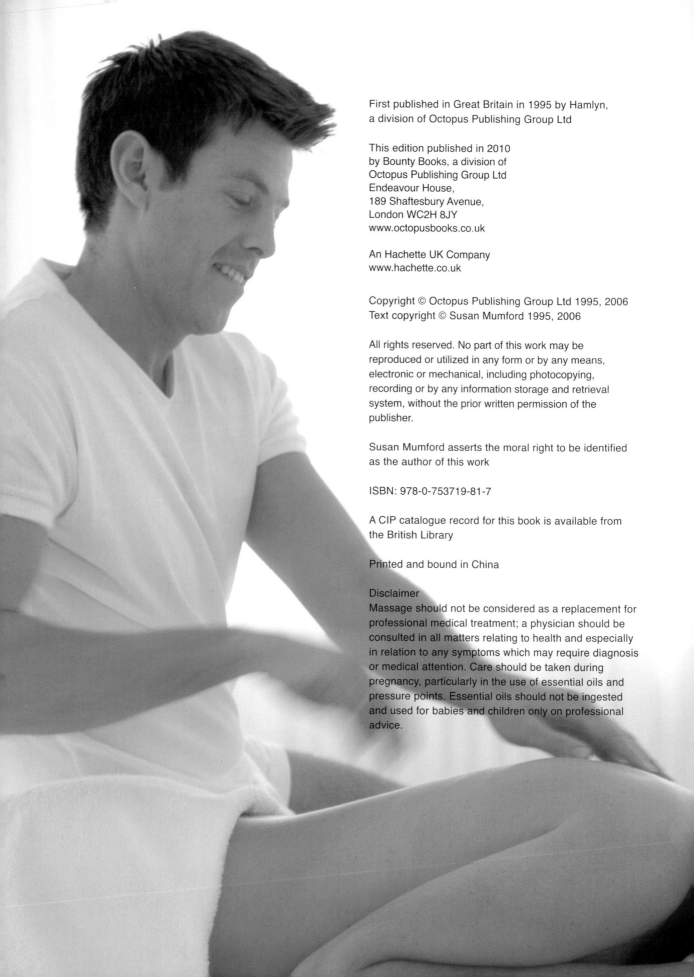

First published in Great Britain in 1995 by Hamlyn,
a division of Octopus Publishing Group Ltd

This edition published in 2010
by Bounty Books, a division of
Octopus Publishing Group Ltd
Endeavour House,
189 Shaftesbury Avenue,
London WC2H 8JY
www.octopusbooks.co.uk

An Hachette UK Company
www.hachette.co.uk

ISBN: 978-0-753719-81-7

A CIP catalogue record for this book is available from
the British Library

Printed and bound in China

Disclaimer
Massage should not be considered as a replacement for
professional medical treatment; a physician should be
consulted in all matters relating to health and especially
in relation to any symptoms which may require diagnosis
or medical attention. Care should be taken during
pregnancy, particularly in the use of essential oils and
pressure points. Essential oils should not be ingested
and used for babies and children only on professional
advice.

contents

introduction 6

before beginning 8
introduction to massage 10
anatomy guide 12
preparation for massage 16

getting started 18
oils 20
a guide to some common oils 22
using oils 24
warming up 26

simple techniques 34
effleurage 36
kneading 38
wringing 40
pulling 42
squeezing 44
opening 45
circling 46
feathering 48
pressing 50
raking 51
stretching 52

simple massage 54
the back 56
the back of the legs 66
the neck 70
the face 72
the arms 74
the chest 78
the abdomen 80
the front of the legs 82

further techniques 86
thumb rolling 88
thumb circling 89
friction 90
heel pressure 92
rocking 94
percussion 96
pressure points 98
the joints 100

further massage 102
the back 104
the back of the legs 114
the feet 118
the neck 120

the face 124
the arms 128
the hands 132
the chest 134
the abdomen 138
front of the legs and feet 142

specific techniques 148
introduction to specific techniques 150
headaches 152
arm relaxation 154
hip and lower back tension 156
sinus problems 158
the abdomen 160
tension headaches 162
facial tension 164
back tension 166
sensual massage 168
self-massage 174

after massage 182
the after-effects of massage 184

index 190
acknowledgements 192

introduction

I am very proud to introduce this new book, updating the original, which has been so popular and translated into many different languages. Since first writing, massage has flourished, becoming so much more widespread and accepted. You can now find different styles of massage in all kinds of exotic locations. But what hasn't changed are the basic dynamics: a pair of hands, an open heart and mind, and a lucky, willing recipient!

The beauty of massage lies in it being such a simple, direct form of human contact. It fulfils the basic need of touching and being touched. Whether it's a fun five-minute back rub or creating an intimate massage space for a friend, your skills can provide genuine release from long-term tension, backache or a dip in confidence. Watch the light creep back into your partner's smile as he or she visibly unravels in front of you! With friends, family and lovers, massage can provide the framework to strengthen your contact and knowledge of each other. If you want to take massage further, and this is certainly where my own interest lies, it can be a very special way of becoming more aware of the deeper levels on which our energies connect and interact with each other.

Massage is a fundamental skill that all of us should have. While it requires learning some basic techniques and strokes, perhaps the most important ingredient is the individuality both of you bring to the experience. At the same time, sensitivity, generosity, warmth and openness are all essential for a massage to mean more than just a series of movements. In fact, an inspired massage is an opportunity for two people to be able to go beyond themselves, nourish the spirit and release creativity. For something that is so simple, massage can have profound and far-reaching effects.

This book is intended to be used as a comprehensive guide to giving a massage. It takes you right through from the very first techniques to the point where you are able to give a full body massage. The massage is presented in two graded stages in order to make it easier to follow, so you can either stop at the simple massage or continue through to the more advanced sequence. In addition, there is a specialized section at the end, which shows specific techniques that can be used to further a massage. First of all, try the massage with a friend you feel comfortable with. Then, if you approach it with a sense of exploration and humour, your discoveries, successes and even your mistakes, can develop and grow into your own personal style.

how to use this book

An introduction to the way the massage progresses through the book may be helpful here. As there is nothing to beat hands-on instruction when you are learning, the massage itself has been presented as closely as possible to how you would actually be taught. You would naturally learn in steps, and certainly not learn everything at once. So, the massage has been divided into clear, easy stages, where you will have the opportunity to complete and practise each stage before going on to the next. Each section builds upon what you have already learned. While you may want to follow each step at first, the idea is for you to develop a collection of strokes from which you can then create your own massage.

In the first section, Before Beginning, there is a basic guide to anatomy and physiology. This helps to give a clear visual idea of exactly where you will be placing your hands. It is intended as background information;

as a theoretical approach to massage can often be more of a hindrance than a help!

The second section, Getting Started, provides a guide to oils and aromatherapy essences, which you can use to enhance the massage, along with some simple recipes to try. Some introductory exercises are then included so that you become more familiar with your own body before working on someone else. Trying the massage strokes on yourself is a helpful exercise before you begin to massage your friend or partner. You will also find some ideas for increasing the sensitivity of your hands. The third section, Simple Techniques, introduces and demonstrates simple massage techniques on several parts of the body, giving a fuller idea of how they can be used. It is best to try these out before you begin.

The next section, Simple Massage, contains a step-by-step guide incorporating the techniques just shown. Follow each step to begin with, then develop your own favourite strokes and style. This massage forms the foundation for the sequence to follow.

The following two sections, Further Techniques and Further Massage, include more advanced techniques, followed by a step-by-step complete body massage. This massage incorporates the new techniques with the strokes and sequence from the simple massage. This not only makes adding the new techniques much easier, but is a great confidence booster! The two massages are followed by Specific Techniques, which includes how to make a massage sensual and self-massage. These have

deliberately not been set out in sequence, but left for you to experiment with and incorporate as you wish. Finally, just as important as starting a massage is the way it ends. After Massage includes making sure you both get the most from the experience, take time to relax afterwards and put back what you have given out.

before beginning

Being at the beginning of something new is always exciting. However, it can appear daunting when you are faced with something large and unknown without really knowing where to begin. Hopefully, by approaching massage in manageable stages, actually beginning will be much easier! The temptation is to want to massage right away, but before going on to the practical aspects, familiarize yourself with this opening section. Having an idea of what you are working with, what you will need to start and why you should massage in the first place all help to give confidence and meaning to what you do. Massage has so many connotations. For whatever reason you decide to massage, the practice has real value and proven results.

introduction to massage

what is massage?

Massage is a form of structured touch. The hands, or sometimes other parts of the body, such as the forearms or elbows, are used to glide over the skin and apply pressure to the underlying muscles in a series of movements that involve variously stroking, rubbing, kneading and pressing. It can be either soothing or stimulating, and when used in conjunction with a focus on energy, can affect the body, mind, spirit and emotions. Massage is an ancient, revered art that has been practised for centuries. The ancient Egyptians, Greeks and Romans all used massage for healing and health, as well as pleasure. In India, China and Japan, massage forms an integral part of whole systems of medicine, while reference to massage in China dates back from between two to three thousand years BC.

what does massage do?

Massage does not actually do anything to the body! However, what it does is to stimulate and encourage the body to carry out its normal functions. In other words, massage is not something you do to another person, it is a process that you initiate, to which the body then responds. Massage provides the stimulation, and the body does the work.

the effects of massage

The therapeutic benefits produced by massage include loosening of muscular tension, toning and firming the muscles, and stimulating the circulation of the blood and lymph. Through too much or not enough exercise, or physical or mental tension, the waste products from muscular activity (carbon dioxide, lactic acid and urea), can accumulate in the muscles, preventing the fibres from sliding easily over each other and producing an increase in muscle tone. Massage aids drainage of these wastes, principally lactic acid, freeing the muscles and restoring normal function. It also reminds the muscles how it feels to be relaxed.

Massage affects nerves as well as muscles. The stimulation of sensory nerve endings in the skin is relayed to the brain via the central nervous system. This acts on the autonomic nervous system to produce a general feeling of relaxation and helps reduce the effects of stress. The relaxation process in turn produces a more natural abdominal breathing pattern which is vital to the functioning of the abdominal organs. Stress and fatigue, caused by the accumulation of waste products, can be reduced, and the metabolic process made more effective. The nervous system also controls the vascular system. A lack of vascular supply results in decreased efficiency in drainage and supply of blood. Stimulation via massage boosts lymph drainage and increases circulation, at the same time improving the appearance of the skin. This has a positive psychological effect. Many skin problems are stress related and one's skin is often a reflection of one's inner state of mind.

Massage helps the body restore its natural balance, is an excellent preventative and, yes, it feels great!

who can benefit?

Massage is for everyone, absolutely. Anyone can massage. It is true that some people have a better natural touch than others, but there is no reason why everyone cannot learn. And anyone can be massaged. There are certain contraindications, but in general everyone can benefit, regardless of their age or physical ability. All of us need touch. It is one of our earliest life experiences and needs.

Touch makes us feel wanted. Without touch we become withdrawn. This is the reason why massage can particularly help people suffering bereavement or loss, or those not in a physical relationship. Touch is a means of communication, affirmation and expression, providing a sense of identity and helping to build confidence and self-esteem. In an increasingly over-stimulated and desensitized world, massage provides the opportunity to keep in touch with our bodies. The all-over glow of being comfortable in our skin is something we often miss out on.

Following a massage, many people will experience the sense of being a connected whole as opposed to a disconnected series of parts. They are also more aware of their physical boundaries and experience the sense of their feet being more firmly planted on the ground. Massage provides that vital and essential sense of touch, of being looked after, without the pressure of having to give back anything in return.

Massage provides balance. If you are feeling over-stimulated, massage can help sedate and calm, or if you are feeling sluggish, it can help wake you up. It can also be used to help specific problems, such as back and shoulder aches, period pains, coughs, headaches and so on, and can be used as part of the process of recuperation after injury or illness. However, be very clear that you are not aiming to cure. *Long-term or acute problems need professional help.* Massage can be used before and after sport or exercise, to help

the body warm up or to relax the muscles afterwards, preventing stiffness the next day. By helping tone the muscles, massage can help as part of a fitness or beauty program, while the use of oils combined with massage will help stimulate cell renewal and improve the elasticity of the skin. Some people worry about their appearance, but in my experience, massage can make you feel much better about your body.

Tension accounts for a lot more problems than we perhaps realize. Most people suffer from one form of stress-related condition or another. This can be felt as physical tension, resulting in tight, knotted muscles, or mental overactivity and anxiety, which will then affect the body function. For anyone who is suffering from stress, massage can help reduce the physical effects of tension and calm the mind and emotions, while restoring vital energy.

The connection between mind and body is such that being in good physical shape affects the mind, and being mentally relaxed helps your body to function better.

anatomy guide

the muscles

Skeletal muscles provide the shape of the body. These are voluntary muscles under conscious control, such as the arms and legs, as opposed to involuntary muscles, which include those of the heart and digestive system.

Each muscle consists of bundles of elastic muscle fibres, each surrounded by cell membrane, bound together by a connective sheath. This is known as the muscle belly. The muscles are primarily attached to the bones at either end by highly resistant connective tissue, or

a guide to the superficial muscles

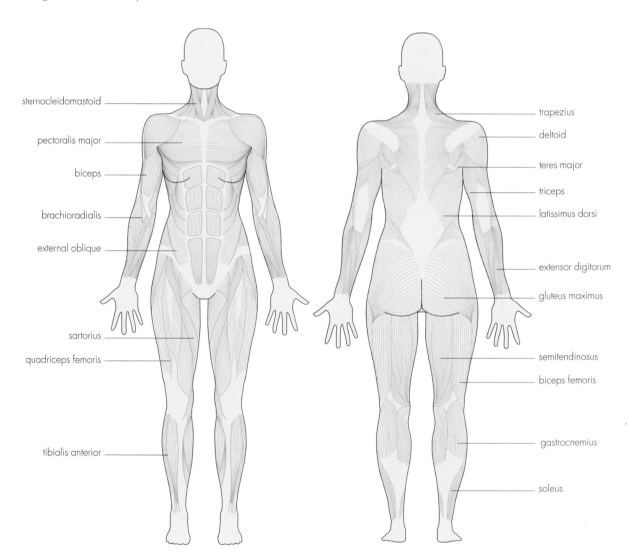

sternocleidomastoid

pectoralis major

biceps

brachioradialis

external oblique

sartorius

quadriceps femoris

tibialis anterior

trapezius

deltoid

teres major

triceps

latissimus dorsi

extensor digitorum

gluteus maximus

semitendinosus

biceps femoris

gastrocnemius

soleus

tendons. The points at which the muscles attach to the bone are known as the origin (the bone the muscle does not move), and the insertion (the bone the muscle does move when it contracts). In normal body function the muscles work in pairs or groups, contracting and relaxing in order to propel the body. Responding to signals from the brain, a muscle will contract. As it does so the fibres slide toward each other, shortening both the length and width of the muscle. This causes movement. The muscle that contracts is called the synergist. The muscles which relax during the same movement are called antagonists. The synergist and antagonist will change depending on the particular movement. When the muscles remain in a contracted state this is known as an increase in resting tone. To function, the muscles need blood containing large amounts of glucose and oxygen and produce, as by-products, the waste materials of carbon dioxide, lactic acid and urea, which are carried away by the venous system and lymph. Where there is a shortening of muscle function, some of this waste may remain in the muscles, causing stiffness, and preventing the fibres from easily sliding over each other.

a guide to the major organs of the body

the lungs
The lungs are spongy structures, protected by the ribs, into which air is drawn. Through the lungs, oxygen enters the bloodstream and carbon dioxide is expired.

the heart
The heart is a muscle. It acts like a pump, contracting to circulate oxygenated blood around the body, and return deoxygenated blood to the lungs.

the liver
The function of the liver is to absorb nutrients from the blood, to break down fats, carbohydrates and proteins, store vitamins and detoxify the blood. It is also concerned with the production of bile.

the large intestine
The large intestine is concerned with the absorption of water, vitamins and minerals, which pass to the liver. The waste products pass through the body.

the kidneys
The kidneys are concerned with the filtering of waste products, and the absorption of water, glucose, protein and vitamins. Their function is to conserve water within the body, and return it to the tissues, the remainder passing through the body as urine.

the stomach
The stomach stores and digests food, breaking it down by means of enzymes in preparation for processing in the small intestine.

the small intestine
The small intestine further breaks down food by means of enzymes and digests sugars, fats and proteins. The majority of nutrients are absorbed here.

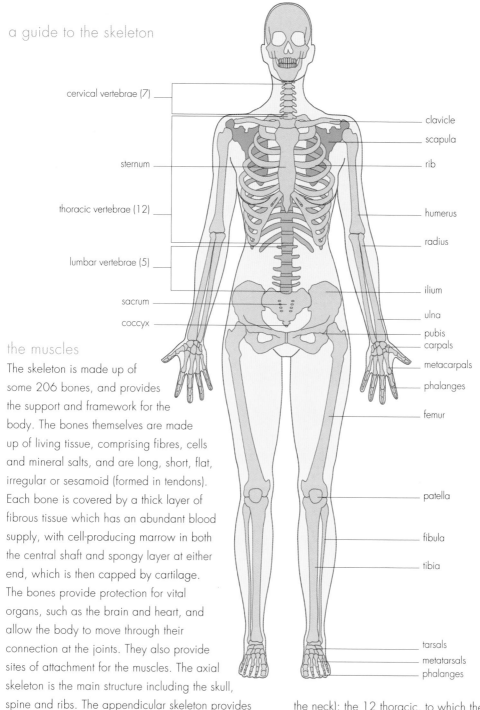

cervical vertebrae (7)

clavicle

scapula

sternum

rib

thoracic vertebrae (12)

humerus

radius

lumbar vertebrae (5)

ilium

sacrum

ulna

coccyx

pubis

carpals

metacarpals

phalanges

femur

patella

fibula

tibia

tarsals

metatarsals

phalanges

the muscles

The skeleton is made up of some 206 bones, and provides the support and framework for the body. The bones themselves are made up of living tissue, comprising fibres, cells and mineral salts, and are long, short, flat, irregular or sesamoid (formed in tendons). Each bone is covered by a thick layer of fibrous tissue which has an abundant blood supply, with cell-producing marrow in both the central shaft and spongy layer at either end, which is then capped by cartilage. The bones provide protection for vital organs, such as the brain and heart, and allow the body to move through their connection at the joints. They also provide sites of attachment for the muscles. The axial skeleton is the main structure including the skull, spine and ribs. The appendicular skeleton provides the supporting framework for the arms and legs, includes the pectoral and pelvic girdles and moves more freely. The vertebrae of the spine are divided into the seven cervical, supporting the neck and skull (the seventh is the bony prominence just below the base of

the neck); the 12 thoracic, to which the ribs are attached; the five lumbar, providing the main support for the body; the five sacral, which are fused together to form the sacrum, distributing the weight of the body to the hips; and the four coccygeal, fused together to form the coccyx.

the ball-and-socket shoulder joint

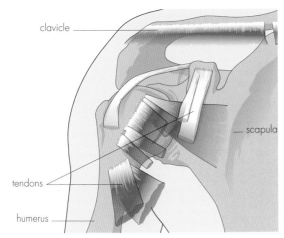

clavicle

scapula

tendons

humerus

the hinge knee joint

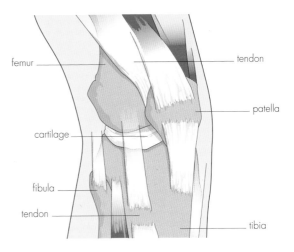

femur

tendon

patella

cartilage

fibula

tendon

tibia

the joints

The point at which two bones connect is a joint. The most common is a synovial joint. Here the bones connect within a cavity surrounded by a fluid-secreting membrane, which protects the cartilage and reduces friction during movement. It is contained by a fibrous capsule and supported by tendons and ligaments. The ball-and-socket type, found at the shoulder and hip, permits a wide range of movement. Here the round head of one bone fits into the socket shape of the other. Hinge joints are found at the elbow and knee. The bone surfaces swing about each other permitting a more limited movement.

the nervous system

The nervous system consists of the central nervous system (the brain and spinal cord) and the peripheral nervous system (the cranial and spinal nerves branching out to all areas of the body). In response to stimuli, sensory receptors in the skin, soft tissue and muscles send impulses via sensory nerves to the central nervous system. Responding to signals from the brain, motor nerves send impulses to the muscles resulting in movement and activity. The autonomic nervous system is concerned with the involuntary movements of the organs, blood vessels and glands. It divides into the sympathetic nervous system, which governs involuntary responses such as increased heartbeat, respiration and

sweat, and the parasympathetic nervous system, which is concerned with a reduction in activity and processes such as digestion and rest. These systems work together to maintain balanced body function.

circulation of the blood

The cardiovascular system consists of the heart, arteries carrying oxygenated blood from the heart, veins returning deoxygenated blood, and capillaries supplying nutrients to the tissues and removing wastes. The blood comprises plasma, red cells supplying oxygen from the lungs to the tissues and cells and removing carbon dioxide, white cells, important to the immune system fighting bacteria and secreting antibodies, and platelets, responsible for clotting. The heart, acting like a pump, has four chambers, two dealing with circulation through the lungs, two with circulation to the rest of the body. Blood in the arteries is pumped at high pressure, the veins operating at lower pressure. In the legs blood flow is assisted by muscle contraction and valves to return blood supply to the heart. The lymph system, arising from the vascular system, helps drain tissues and return fluid to the heart. The lymph flows through its own vessel system, draining into ducts. Nodes or glands filter the fluid, producing lymphocites to neutralize bacteria. Flow is aided by muscle contraction.

preparation for massage

where to massage.

In theory, you can massage anywhere. It all depends on the type of massage you are giving. If you are adapting your massage for a quick neck and shoulder or hand massage, for example, you can simply do it wherever you happen to be. However, do follow the basic principles so that your partner is sitting with a supported back, either on the floor or on a chair, and make sure they do not slouch by supporting the forehead or chest with your hand if necessary. You can then massage outdoors, in the office or wherever. It is equally important that you massage from a comfortable position, without having to twist or strain. If, however, you are giving a full body massage, you need to choose your location a little more carefully. You will need to find a place where there is enough room for your partner to lie flat and for you to be able to move around them, and somewhere preferably that is quiet, comfortable and warm, where you will not be disturbed. A living room or bedroom floor is fine. However, the massage surface needs to be firm enough so that your partner will be supported and not sink into it, so do not massage on the bed as this is far too soft. If you are planning to do a lot of massage, then it is worth investing in a massage table. This is less intimate, but will also be less of a strain on your back.

The importance of your posture cannot be overemphasized. As well as avoiding a strain on your muscles, keeping the spine relaxed but straight as you perform the movements will significantly enhance your massage. It is also worth mentioning that as you are the person giving the massage, you need to be in a place where you feel comfortable. If you are happier in your own home, where you will have your things to hand, know what kind of coming and going there will be,

and can keep an eye on the time, then ask your partner to travel to you.

the best time to massage

Again, this depends on the massage. The best time is ideally when you are feeling fresh and enthusiastic. Some people prefer to give or have a massage in the morning, others prefer later in the day. A neck and shoulder massage can be done at almost any time, on the spot if you are happy to do it. A body massage can be almost as flexible, taking certain points into consideration. Avoid massaging after a heavy meal. This applies especially to your partner, as the system is busy digesting food and the pressure can feel uncomfortable. In the same way, do not drink alcohol before or immediately after a massage. Drinking before a massage dulls its effect, speeds up the absorption process and can make you feel sick. Directly after a massage also has a negative effect, and the alcohol will affect you much more quickly. (Massage can actually help with the effects of a mild hangover by helping to clear the system. However, if it is severe, the body will be far too sensitive.)

You should plan your massage when both of you have free time and do not have to rush. This means setting aside at least 90 minutes (up to an hour for a longer massage and a good 15 minutes either side). You also need to take into account the effects that massage has. If your partner has to go to work, a deep relaxation massage would be unsuitable. Some people do indeed like to have a massage before work or in a lunchbreak, to relax before an important performance or to get in shape before a run. This is fine as long as you adapt your massage to more stimulating strokes. It is also important you know this beforehand. As always, you must take your own needs into account. Do not massage late at night, as this will be too stimulating. While massage can help transform your state of mind, if you are preoccupied, busy, tired or in a bad mood, this is not the time for you to give out any more of your energy.

what you will need

In order for the massage to go smoothly, have everything laid out beforehand. You will need a comfortable but firm surface for your partner to lie on, so start with a foam mat or small futon, for example, on the floor. You could even use a folded duvet or sleeping bag. You will then need a sheet to cover your surface, towels to cover your partner, pillows or cushions for the head or legs and possibly a cushion for you to kneel on. You will need the oil at room temperature, extra heating available if necessary, soft lighting, some tissues to wipe off excess oil and somewhere to wash your hands. If you have an answer machine, remember to switch it on. It is also a good idea to have a clock and set a time limit before you start. When you begin to massage, especially, you can easily run over time, which is tiring for you, and your partner may be wondering when the massage is going to end! Add your own personal touches to make your massage room inviting, such as flowers, an aromatherapy burner or music. These may seem like small points, but attention to detail makes all the difference and means you can both put all your concentration into the massage.

before you start

Before you begin to massage, agree a time limit with your partner and make sure you know if they have to go to work afterwards or, for example, do not want oil near their hair or face. Next, you need to ask a few questions before the massage begins. Check your partner's health and make sure you know about any current illnesses, medication or on-going problems such as neck or shoulder tension. Find out if there are particular parts of the body they would like massaged,

or if there are any areas you should avoid. Even if you know your partner well, do not miss this stage out.

contraindications

This means the circumstances in which you need to be careful or should not massage at all. In general, as long as you are sensitive, you will not do any harm.

pregnancy: Massage during pregnancy can feel wonderful. However, at all stages of pregnancy, you should only work gently. Avoid massaging over the abdomen during the first four months, simply rest your hands instead, and thereafter circle very lightly. Check the list of essential oils carefully. Depending on the stage of pregnancy, you will need to adapt your partner's massage position.

injuries: Do not massage directly over recent scar tissue, injuries, sprains, open cuts or wounds. These will heal by themselves. However, gentle massage around the injury can be helpful.

illnesses: Do not massage directly over a tumour, skin rash or massage if your partner has a heart condition. Massage can actually be very good for the heart, but seek professional advice first. If in doubt, always consult your doctor or a health professional beforehand.

varicose veins: Do not massage over varicose veins, but simply brush your hands over the leg lightly instead.

pains: Be practical. Never try to cure. If your partner has persistent aches, pains, muscular or spinal problems or experiences any sharp pain during massage, consult your doctor.

Finally, to make sure your movements feel smooth, remove your jewellery (your partner should do the same), and make sure you have filed nails. Strong perfume can also interfere with your partner's enjoyment. Always wash your hands before and after each massage.

getting started

A good massage needs a little careful thought and preparation. The amount of effort you put in will never be lost. The use of oils is exhilarating, but again you need some background information before you start. First get a feel for the oils, then you can begin to experiment. Similarly, trying out the strokes on yourself and finding out more about your own body are an inevitable part of the massage process. The more you know about yourself, and the more attention you pay to developing the feeling in your hands, the more successful your massages will be. Not only do you learn more, but your partner will feel your enthusiasm and directly benefit from all your time and effort.

oils

Part of the preparation for massage is the selection and use of oils. The purpose of using oil is to help your hands move over your partner's body without pulling or stretching the skin. Most people like the feel of oil, although you do not absolutely have to use it. Some use talcum powder, and some strokes can be done through the clothes. However, if you choose to use oils, it is a good idea to have a selection prepared before you start.

The basic oil is called a base or carrier oil, and this is generally a vegetable or nut oil. You can use mineral oil, but this is not easily absorbed by the skin. The most popular carrier oils are grapeseed or sweet almond. Personally, I find almond oil is a little too cloying, and prefer grapeseed with about five or ten per cent almond oil added. Carrot, apricot or peach kernel, avocado, wheatgerm and jojoba oils, which are much richer, can also be used. They are not recommended over large areas, but are excellent mixed in with other oils. A teaspoonful of wheatgerm oil can be used as an antioxidant to preserve your mixtures.

These oils can then be used as carriers for essential oils. This means that they can be used to dissolve the essential oils, helping them penetrate the skin. (This takes around 30 minutes.) Again you do not need to use the essences, but they are delightful and enhance the massage. Essential oils are the essences of plants that are extracted principally by means of steam distillation. Each oil contains the life force, quality and personality of the plant in concentrated form. The oil is produced by glands within the plant, be it in the leaves, roots or flowers, and it is this essence that is extracted. The oils are highly concentrated and potent, and should never be used directly on the skin as they

will cause irritation. In too high a concentration they may have their opposite effect. Each oil has a rate of volatility, or rate at which it will evaporate, and these categories are divided into top, middle and base notes. The top notes have a high rate of volatility, and a higher vibration. They tend to have an immediate effect on the mind and are generally quickening and uplifting. Middle notes are used to help the organs and functions of the body, while the base notes are sedative in effect and can be used to anchor the top notes in a mixture. Essential oils can be used separately, but when mixed they interact with each other, enhancing and changing the quality of the whole. You usually use between two and four oils in any mixture; when using four have at least one middle note. While aromatherapy is an art in itself, essential oils can successfully be used to create certain moods, to stimulate or relax and, as long as you are not relying on them as cures in any sense, can be used to help with minor ailments, such as blocked sinuses, skin irritations and aching muscles.

The use of oils is very personal. They affect us through their odour, as well as being absorbed through the skin. Smell is one of the most primitive brain functions and one of the most evocative. Therefore, in mixing oils, preference plays a great part and is very much a matter of what feels right. If you or your partner do not like a smell, there is no point in using it. Similarly, as you massage you will naturally absorb oil through your hands, so if an oil affects you adversely, you should simply stop using it immediately. Use the oils sparingly, with just enough for your hands and the amount your partner's skin can absorb.

a guide to some common oils and their properties

base oils

grapeseed A light, inexpensive carrier oil. Excellent for general use. Can be used on its own or as the base for a mixture.

sweet almond Another popular and widely used carrier oil. It can be used on its own or as the base for a mixture.

apricot or peach kernel Light oils, particularly good for the face. Use as part of a mixture.

avocado A rich oil, one of the most penetrative and easily absorbed. Particularly good for dry skin. Use as part of a mixture.

carrot Rich in vitamin A. Also good for the face, but not always widely available. Only use in small amounts as part of a mixture.

jojoba A form of vegetable wax. It is very rich and relatively expensive – best used on the face.

wheatgerm A rich oil, excellent for dry skin. It has a high vitamin E content, and is good for scar tissue and stretch marks. Use as part of a mixture and as an antioxidant. *Do not use if you or your partner have a wheat allergy.*

Most vegetable oils, such as olive, may be used, but ensure the smell is not too strong.

essential oils

basil (top note) Basil is an antiseptic and nerve tonic. It is good for catarrh, sinus congestion, bronchitis and indigestion. It has an uplifting effect, clearing the mind and relieving mental fatigue. *Avoid during pregnancy.*

bergamot (top note) Bergamot is an antiseptic, good for vaginal infections, cystitis, bronchitis, bad breath and sore throats. It is sedative and at the same time uplifting, helpful for anxiety and depression. (*Do not use directly on the skin or when in direct sunlight.*)

camomile (middle note) Camomile is good for soothing inflammation and is useful for ulcers, burns, diarrhea and migraines. It also relieves muscular aches. It can be used for painful or heavy periods and on dry or sensitive skin. It is sedative and anti-depressant, calming the mind and nerves.

clary sage (middle note) Clary sage is a nerve tonic and a sedative, especially good for nervous depression. It eases menstrual cramps and promotes labour. It is useful for inflamed skin conditions and is mildly euphoric. *Avoid during pregnancy.* (Use sparingly.)

frankincense (base note) Frankincense is an astringent and is useful for coughs, catarrh, cystitis and vaginal infections. It rejuvenates the skin and has a soothing effect on the mind. It is safe to use during pregnancy.

geranium (base note) Geranium is a skin cleanser and tonic, as well as a mild diuretic. It is helpful for pains, burns, skin inflammation, diarrhea and ulcers, and can be used to provide hormonal balance during the menopause. It sedates and uplifts, and is useful in anxiety states.

jasmine (base note) Jasmine is an anti-spasmodic, sedative and anti-depressant. It relieves menstrual cramps, promotes childbirth, is useful for coughs and catarrh, and can be used for dry skin conditions. It has a relaxing, uplifting, euphoric effect. *Best avoided during the first months of pregnancy.*

juniper (middle note) Juniper is a nerve tonic, has a sedating effect and is useful in states of stress and anxiety. It is a diuretic, blood purifier, skin tonic and mild astringent, and may be used for rheumatism, cystitis, indigestion, flatulence, eczema and oily skin. *Avoid during pregnancy.*

lavender (middle note) Lavender is one of the most useful oils of all. It is an antiseptic, relieves skin inflammation and is excellent for burns and scalds (you can apply it directly on unbroken skin). It is also good for rheumatism, cystitis and diarrhea. It relieves nausea, headaches, vomiting, cramps and promotes childbirth. It is also good for muscular aches and pains. It is sedative and relaxing, relieving depression and nervous tension. If you only have one oil, this is the one to have.

marjoram (middle note) Marjoram is a sedative and nerve tonic. A warming and comforting oil, it is useful for insomnia. It aids digestion, relieves muscle spasm and lowers blood pressure. It can be used for colds, headaches, constipation and painful periods. *Avoid during pregnancy.*

neroli (base note) Neroli is sedative, anti-depressant and calming, excellent for insomnia, palpitations, anxiety and depression. It is also good for diarrhoea. It regenerates the skin and can be used on dry, irritated skin.

patchouli (base note) Patchouli is a stimulant and astringent. It aids mental clarity, can be used on irritated, cracked or ageing skin, and is useful for water retention, diarrhoea and constipation.

rose (base note) Rose is an antiseptic. It is cleansing, soothing, promotes circulation, strengthens the digestive system, relieves constipation and normalizes menstrual flow. It is useful for mature, dry skin. As an anti-depressant, it can be used for nervous tension and stress relief, and is useful when suffering from grief.

rosemary (middle note) Rosemary is an antiseptic and stimulant, acts as a heart tonic and relieves coughs and colds, headaches, stomach aches, palpitations and diarrhoea. It aids mental clarity and memory loss, and has a beneficial effect on the eyes. It acts as a cleanser and is good for dandruff and toning the skin. It also relieves muscular aches and pains. *Best avoided during pregnancy.*

sandalwood (base note) Sandalwood stimulates the digestion, is useful for diarrhoea, sore throats, catarrh and coughs. It is an antiseptic, effective in respiratory and urinary infections and excellent for relieving dry, inflamed skin. As a sedative, it can be used for nervous tension and anxiety.

ylang-ylang (base note) Ylang-ylang is a sedative and euphoric and is used for anxiety and nervous tension. It lowers the blood pressure and is good for oily skin. (Use sparingly.)

using oils

Keep the base oils separate from the essential oils until you are ready to make up a mixture. To make up a bottle of oil, you will need about 50 ml (2 fl oz) of base oil. To this, add up to, but not more than, 25 drops of essential oil. This will be enough for six to eight massages. For a smaller quantity, halve the amounts. Kept in a dark, stoppered glass bottle in a cool place, the mixture should last between six to eight weeks. For one massage, you can use a couple of drops of essence added to a small bowl of oil.

Once you have chosen and mixed the oil it should be warmed before you massage, and applied by pouring a little onto your hands, never onto your partner's skin. (*Note: Be careful around the eyes. Essential oils can sting.*) Essential oils need to be pure. They are expensive because of the extraction process and the quantities needed to produce them – but they do last a long time.

For therapeutic purposes, always make sure you obtain the highest quality (absolute) of oils such as rose and jasmine. The advantage is they smell wonderful and you will only need small quantities, so the expense balances out. Essential oils can be used in other ways, in baths, as inhalations or burned. A delightful addition to a massage is to scent the room with oils before you begin.

recipes

Listed below and opposite are some recipes you might like to try out before experimenting with your own. All of the ingredients are readily available. Do remember that certain oils will tend to blend together better than others, and that when you are starting off, it is better to use them one at a time. The recipes are intended as an introductory guide only. *In order to treat conditions, you should always seek professional advice.*

base oils

base oil
For 50 ml (2 fl oz) base oil:
Grapeseed oil 95%
Almond oil 5%
Half tsp wheatgerm oil (optional)

rich base oil
Grapeseed oil 95%
Avocado oil 5%
Half tsp wheatgerm oil (optional)

luxury base oil
Almond oil 90%
Apricot or peach kernel oil 10%
Half tsp wheatgerm oil (optional)

essential oils to be diluted in 50 ml (2 fl oz) base oil

stimulating oil
Lavender 15 drops
Rosemary 10 drops
This is good for relaxing the
muscles and clearing the system.

soothing oil
Camomile 15 drops
Lavender 10 drops
This helps nervous tension,
headaches and dry, flaky,
irritated skin.

warming, stimulating oil
Rosemary 12 drops
Marjoram 8 drops
Basil 5 drops
This stimulates the system
and is good for colds.

uplifting and refreshing oil
Rosemary 12 drops
Bergamot 9 drops
Geranium 4 drops
This oil relieves nervous
tension and mental fatigue.

fragrant, soothing oil
Rose Absolute 5 drops
Neroli 5 drops
Geranium 5 drops
This smells wonderful, is
calming and very good for stress.

relaxing oil
Lavender 12 drops
Geranium 8 drops
Sandalwood 5 drops
This is a sedating oil.

relaxing oil
Neroli 11 drops
Lavender 9 drops
Camomile 5 drops
Sedating, will help you sleep.

stimulating oil
Rosemary 11 drops
Lavender 9 drops
Juniper 5 drops
This helps cleanse the system
and is good for cellulite.

soothing oil
Frankincense 16 drops
Rose Absolute 9 drops
This is great for the skin. (*Note:*
Safe to use after the fourth month
of pregnancy.)

uplifting oil
Basil 11 drops
Jasmine Absolute 9 drops
This breaks the middle note
rule, but smells truly delightful!

heady, soothing oil
Lavender 14 drops
Frankincense 7 drops
Sandalwood 4 drops
This is an antiseptic oil, excellent
for the skin and good for catarrh.

rich, soothing oil
Lavender 9 drops
Frankincense 6 drops
Rose Absolute 6 drops
Patchouli 4 drops
This is luxurious, relaxing
and good for mature, dry skin.

warming up

Before massaging a partner, I recommend trying out some movements on your own body first, so that you can experiment with techniques and pressure and feel free to make mistakes! On the following pages are some simple exercises through which you can explore the way your body moves and how the movements feel, plus a few warm-ups for your hands. Warming up before a massage is essential. The exciting thing about massage is that it is not only about using your hands, it involves using your energy as well. Follow the steps to stimulate the flow of energy through your fingers before the first massage contact. To put your partner at ease, have complete confidence in your touch.

relaxed breathing Lie on your back, knees bent and the lower back flat against the floor. Place both hands over your abdomen and breathe naturally. Empty your mind, focusing simply on the rise and fall of your belly.

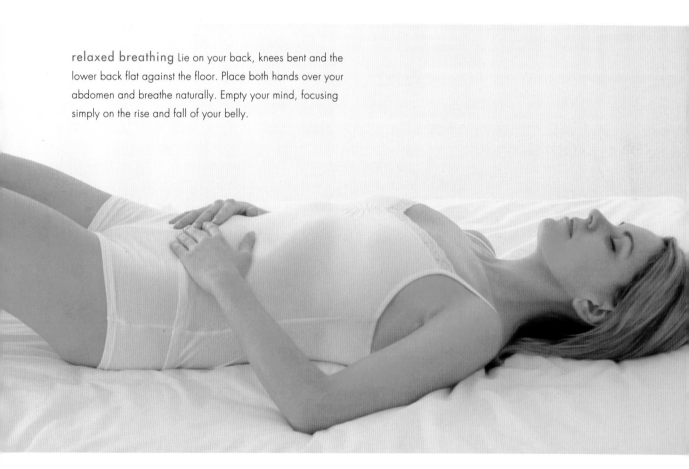

turning the head Sit in a comfortable position with your back straight. Turn your head slowly to the right as far as possible and then to the left. Keep your shoulders still. Notice which muscles are involved in the movement, how far your head can comfortably turn and any difference you feel afterwards.

forward head tilt Slowly tilt your head forward, chin toward your chest and back straight. Focus on the muscles. Feel how flexible they are and at which point you feel a strain. Slowly raise your head up to the centre again.

backward head tilt Very slowly tilt your head right back, as far as feels comfortable. Keep your mouth and jaw relaxed so that your throat feels open. Feel the movement from inside and notice any point at which you tense. Try doing this with your jaw tight and feel the difference it makes.

relaxing the jaw Notice how you hold your jaw when your mouth is closed. Feel if the muscles are loose or clenched. Open your mouth, slowly dropping your jaw and consciously relaxing the muscles. Keep your mouth relaxed and notice if this feels new to you. Yawn if you want – it's a sign of letting go!

stretching Either sitting or standing with a straight back, reach upward with one arm, stretching as far as you can. Then, stretch up with the other arm, each time reaching a little higher. Notice which muscles are doing the work.

flexing the hip Lie comfortably on your back. Slowly bring your knee toward your chest, clasping your leg to help the stretch. Feel the muscles involved in the movement, breathe out, relax and make the stretch a little tighter. Now do the same on the other leg, noting any difference in their flexibility.

flexing the foot With one leg straight out in front of you, flex your foot, bringing the toes back toward you. Watch the muscles work and really feel the stretch down the back of your leg. Breathe out, relax and flex some more. Notice the feeling this leaves you with and the way your muscles feel afterwards.

tensing the forearms Holding your arms out in front of you, form your hands into fists and tense the muscles as hard as you can. Feel how far the tension spreads and the way in which your body is affected. Breathe out and release. Notice how your muscles feel immediately afterwards. Tense and release several times.

opening the hands Make your hands into loose fists and hold them in this position for a moment. Then, quickly open your hands right out, stretching your thumbs and fingers as wide as you can. Repeat several times. Notice any different feelings in your hands. This is a good movement for flexibility.

finger wave Hold your hands in a relaxed position in front of you and then, leading with the little fingers, bring them all down, one after the other, toward the heels of your hands. Start again when the fingers reach the heel, so it is a continuous wave. This exercise is great for keeping the fingers light and flexible.

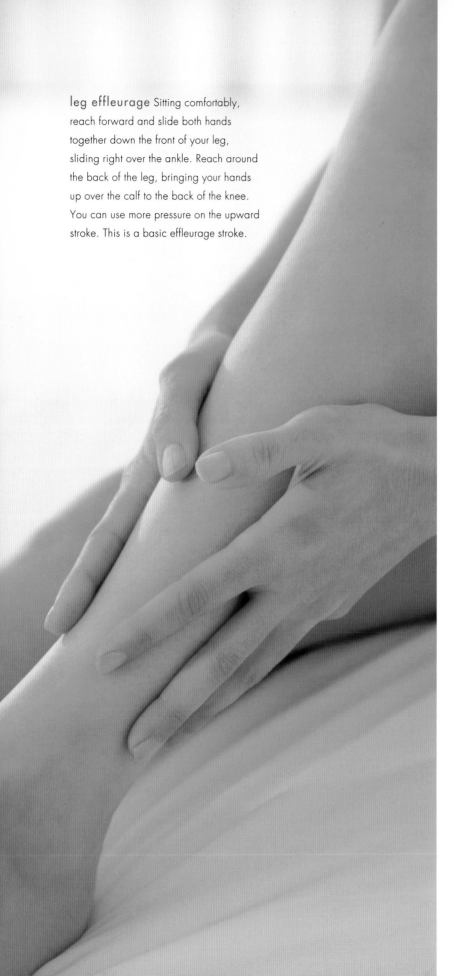

leg effleurage Sitting comfortably,
reach forward and slide both hands
together down the front of your leg,
sliding right over the ankle. Reach around
the back of the leg, bringing your hands
up over the calf to the back of the knee.
You can use more pressure on the upward
stroke. This is a basic effleurage stroke.

twisting the fingers Rest your
hand in a relaxed position. Place the
thumb and forefinger of the other
hand at either side of the base of your
finger. Twist the flesh away from you
with forefinger and thumb. Twist up
until you reach the tip of each finger,
varying the pressure and speed.

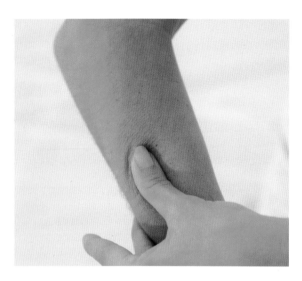

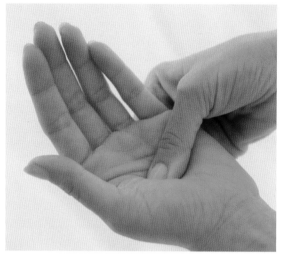

circling the forearm Relax your forearm. Place your thumb in the centre, roughly between the two forearm bones, and make small circling movements on the spot, using the pad of the thumb. Circle on the spot at intervals down toward the wrist, experimenting with different pressures.

pressing the hand Rest one hand palm upward and support it with your other hand. Place your thumb in the centre of the palm and simply press downward, then release. Continue pressing over the entire palm, trying out the movement at different speeds. Use the length, pad and tip of the thumb to vary the stroke.

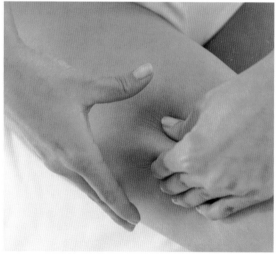

hacking the thigh Raise your leg slightly and with your hands positioned sideways to the leg, chop down lightly on the thigh and then lift your hand up again. Hack with alternate hands, keeping your fingers relaxed and open. The movements, however, should be sharp and snappy. Hack quickly over the thigh.

kneading the thigh Sit in a position that allows you to easily reach your thigh. With one hand grasp a roll of muscle, pressing in with your thumb and pushing it away from you. Then roll it back toward you with your fingers. Knead the thigh with alternate hands, finding the areas where the stroke is most effective.

3 stimulating energy When massaging you need to feel, or imagine, that the energy is coming from the centre of your body out toward your hands. Relax and breathe naturally. As you breathe out, feel the energy moving up from your abdomen through your body and then out through the palms of your hands.

1 stimulating energy Before massaging, you need to sensitize your hands and stimulate your energy. To practise this, sit or stand in a relaxed position and begin rubbing your hands together vigorously. Feel the heat that is generated, particularly in the palms of your hands. Continue to rub for a few moments.

2 stimulating energy Draw both hands apart to about shoulderwidth, and then slowly move them back toward each other again. When you are conscious of a sensation between the hands, stop for a moment, almost as if you are holding an invisible ball. Explore it by moving your hands apart and together again.

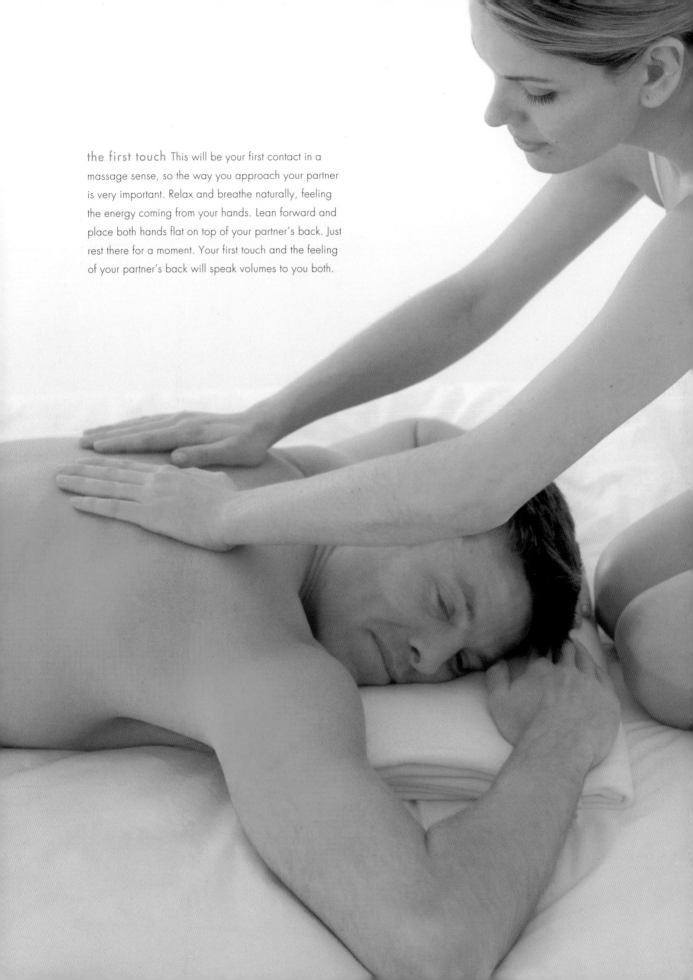

the first touch This will be your first contact in a
massage sense, so the way you approach your partner
is very important. Relax and breathe naturally, feeling
the energy coming from your hands. Lean forward and
place both hands flat on top of your partner's back. Just
rest there for a moment. Your first touch and the feeling
of your partner's back will speak volumes to you both.

simple techniques

The following techniques will provide you with the foundation for your first massage. These movements include effleurage, and kneading and squeezing – strokes which will always be included in any massage, as well as the softer, soothing strokes. Try out the techniques first as part of the massage preparation, becoming familiar with the parts of the body they are used on, as well as when they are used. As you practise, begin to get a feel for the amount of pressure needed. It will differ from person to person and depend on the area you are working on. Always make sure your own position is comfortable. You now have the essential ingredients for giving a massage at your fingertips.

effleurage

Effleurage is the first massage stroke. It is used to spread oil over the body and to prepare your partner by relaxing the surface of the muscles. It also gives you a chance to 'feel out' any areas of tension before you begin. Effleurage strokes are always very gentle, relaxing and reassuring. Effleurage each area with warm, oiled hands before massaging. (Never pour oil directly on the body.) Use large, sweeping strokes to cover the entire area, with greater pressure as you work toward the heart, and lighter on the downward stroke. Keep your hands relaxed and mould them to the shape of your partner's muscles. Effleurage is soothing and can always be used to fill in if you feel unsure of your strokes.

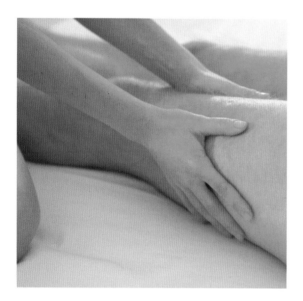

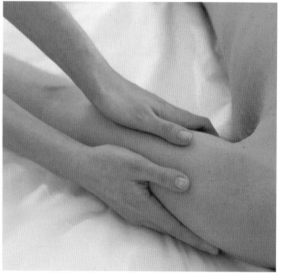

the legs Rub some oil onto your hands. Place the hands together over the ankle, then glide up the front of the calf, around the knee and up over the front of the thigh. Separate your hands at the top of the thigh, reach up to the hip with the outer hand and return down the outside of the leg, using a lighter pressure.

the arms Rub some oil over your hands. Place the fingertips together over the wrist and slide up the centre of the arm, reaching right up over the shoulder. Then, separate your hands and draw them lightly down the outside of the arm returning to the wrist. Mould your hands closely to the shape of your partner's muscles and joints.

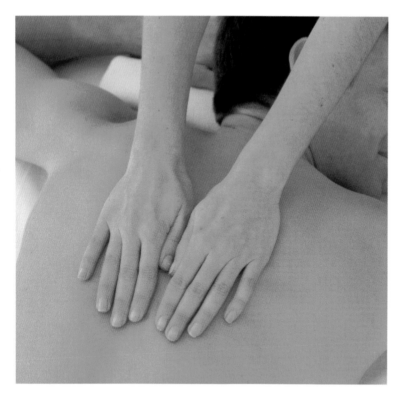

the back Oil your hands and position them together at the top of the back, fingertips pointing downward. Glide down over the muscles as far as you can reach, separating your hands over the lower back. Fan out to the side of the body, bringing your hands back up the sides of the ribs and around the shoulder blades to your original position. Stroke lightly off the neck or arms.

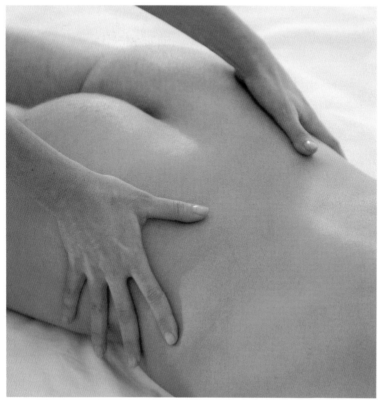

lower back and hips Rub some oil onto your hands. Place them together in the centre of the lower back, fingertips together. Circle upward, then spread your hands and fan outward over the hips. Slide around the hips and continue the circling motion back up over the buttocks. Return to the lower back, bringing your fingertips together once more.

kneading

Kneading is a movement that really is a bit like kneading dough. It is done with the hands working alternately, squeezing and rolling the muscles. It is best used over soft, fleshy areas, like the buttocks and thighs, but can also be used over smaller areas, such as the shoulders or pectorals. The strokes can be done quite firmly, applying extra pressure with the thumbs, but avoid kneading directly over the bone. Make sure that the muscles you are working on are adequately oiled. Too little and you may pinch or pull the skin, too much and your hands will slide. Put your body weight behind the strokes, so the movements do not simply come from your hands. This is a deep, releasing movement used after strokes to prepare the muscles, and it will loosen and disperse tension effectively.

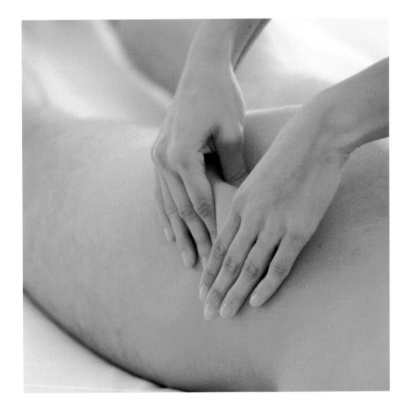

the buttocks You can knead quite firmly over this soft, muscular area. Lean over your partner. Press into the muscles with your thumb and push away from you as you do so. Then, roll the muscles back toward you with your fingers. Repeat the movement with the other hand, working in a gentle rhythm.

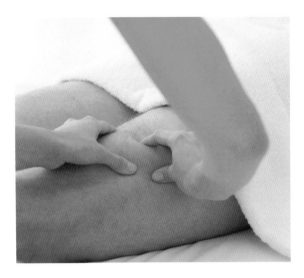

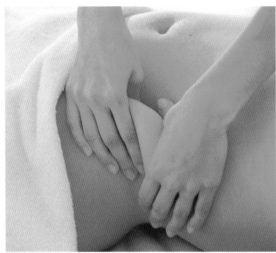

the thighs Place your hands over the muscles at the back of the thigh. Push away from you with your thumb, rolling the muscles back with your fingers, and continue the movement using your hands alternately. Knead over the thigh, but work only on the muscular areas, avoiding the inner thigh, knee and hip.

the abdomen Lean over your partner. Grasp a roll of flesh at the side of the abdomen, between the rib cage and hip. Press in with your thumb and roll with the fingers, alternating the movement with your other hand. Keep the strokes small. Be careful not to dig in too much, or work directly over the abdomen.

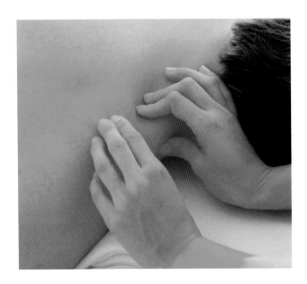

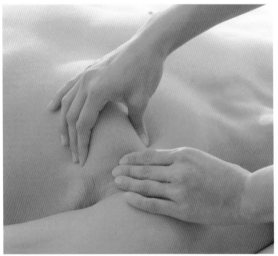

the shoulders Grasp the muscles that run along the top of the shoulder. Press in with your thumb, rolling back toward you with your fingertips. Knead along the shoulder to the neck and back. Again, your movements will have to be quite tight. Squeeze and roll the muscles firmly to ease and loosen any tension.

the chest Place your hands over the pectoral muscles. Press in with the thumb and roll back with the fingers. Knead the area with your hands alternately, keeping your movements precise. Do not knead over the nipples, and for a woman, avoid the breasts. Squeeze and lift the muscles for extra release.

wringing

Wringing involves a pushing and pulling, twisting movement of the hands in opposite directions, which has the effect of pressing the muscles in between the hands as they move toward each other. It is used after kneading and squeezing strokes when the muscles have been loosened, and is often used to return the hands from one area of the body to another. The strokes are as satisfying to perform as to receive. As the flesh twists, you can almost feel the tension being wrung and drained from the muscles. Wringing is used in a series of continuous movements on fleshy areas, where there is a good bulk of muscle to work with. However, with lighter pressure, it can be used over the arms as well.

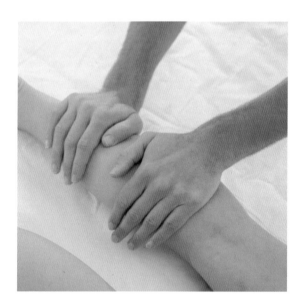

the calves Place both hands over the back of the calf, one hand on the side nearest to you, the other on the far side. Push away from you with your near hand, at the same time pulling back toward you with the other. Twist the muscles as your hands cross and continue the stroke up and down the calf.

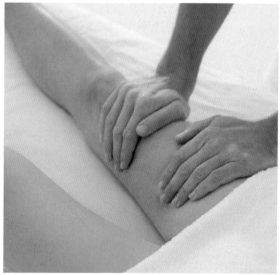

the thighs Place both hands on either side of your partner's thigh, fingers pointing away from you. Push away from you with one hand, drawing back toward you with the other. Continue the movement as the hands cross, ending up again on opposite sides. Wring firmly over the thigh several times.

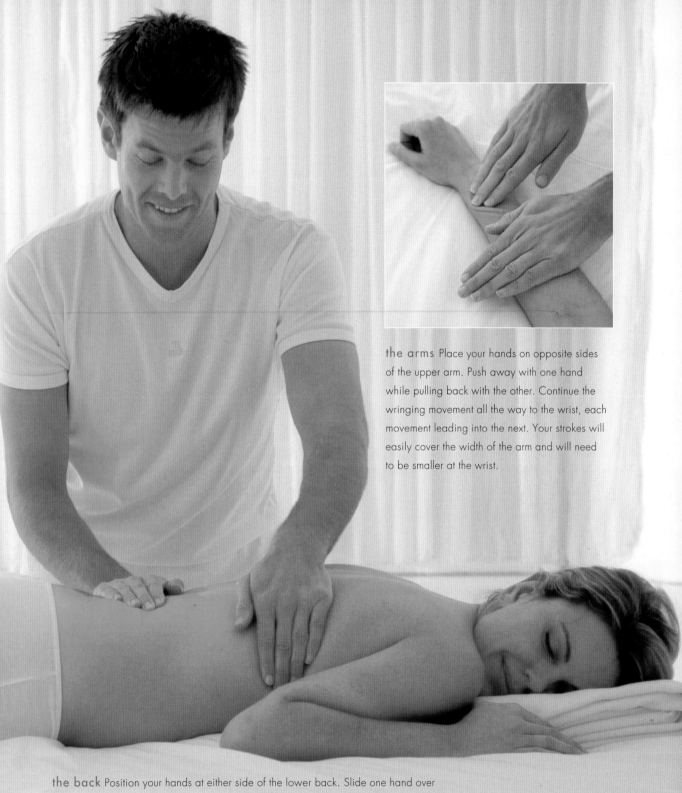

the arms Place your hands on opposite sides of the upper arm. Push away with one hand while pulling back with the other. Continue the wringing movement all the way to the wrist, each movement leading into the next. Your strokes will easily cover the width of the arm and will need to be smaller at the wrist.

the back Position your hands at either side of the lower back. Slide one hand over toward the centre of the back, while pulling the other in the opposite direction. Use a firm pressure to twist the muscles in the middle. Continue the movement until your hands have reached opposite sides. Now, wring slightly further up and continue the movement up toward the shoulders and then back again.

pulling

Pulling is a releasing stroke used to loosen up a whole area rather than a specific group of muscles and is generally used after kneading. As you perform the stroke you pull against the body weight, so that it moves with your hands. The hands should be kept soft and rounded, beginning the strokes just beneath the body. As they slide up and over, so you release the muscles. Pulling is always done up the sides of the body, rolling the muscles as you work, and can be used to move from one area to another. You can pull the hands, one after the other, for example, at the abdomen, or travel along the body, hands crossing over as you move. Pulling can always be used when you are not sure of your next stroke.

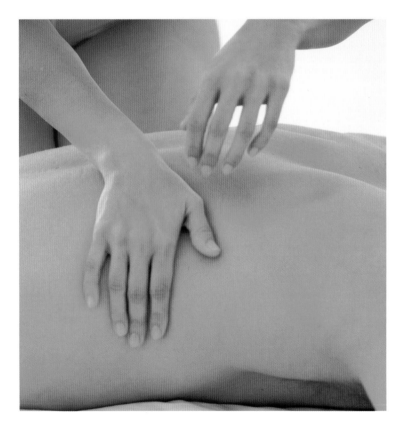

the back Lean across your partner, placing one hand under the body, just above the hip. Now, keeping close in to the body shape, pull your hand up and back toward you, lifting lightly off at the end. Follow this with your other hand slightly further up. Continue pulling, with hands crossing over, up the back.

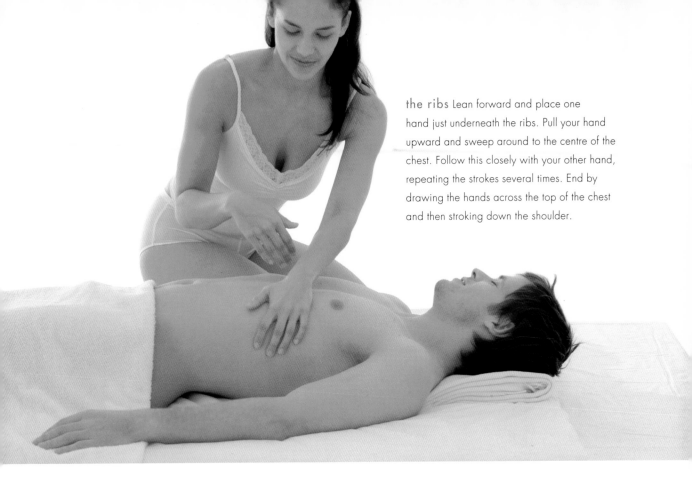

the ribs Lean forward and place one hand just underneath the ribs. Pull your hand upward and sweep around to the centre of the chest. Follow this closely with your other hand, repeating the strokes several times. End by drawing the hands across the top of the chest and then stroking down the shoulder.

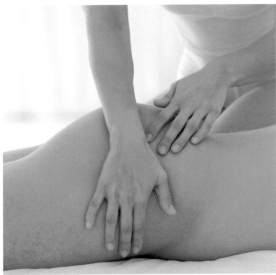

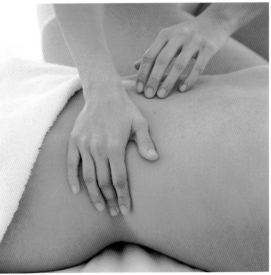

the hips Lean across your partner. Place one hand under the hip and draw up and back toward you over the buttock, repeating the movement with your other hand. Pull with alternate hands several times. The body should rock with your strokes. Move up and down over the hips. End by lightly lifting your hands away.

the abdomen Lean over your partner and place one hand underneath the body, between the rib cage and hip. Pull back toward you, drawing your hand over the abdomen. Follow this with your other hand, repeating the movements several times. This feels particularly good the further under the body you are able to reach.

squeezing

Generally the first stroke performed after effleurage, using one or both hands, it is used to tightly squeeze the muscles, loosening tension in preparation for further releasing strokes. Squeezing the limbs is always done up the body toward the heart. Cover the entire length of the muscles in order to get the best results, always easing pressure as you approach the joints.

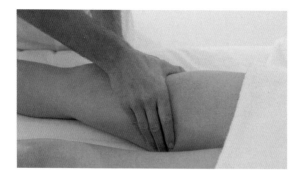

the thighs Position your hands above the knee, thumbs to one side of the thigh muscles, fingers to the other. Squeeze upward, spreading your hands as wide as possible. Push up to the top of the thigh, separate your hands and round off over the hip. Repeat in strips up the thigh.

the calves Place both hands over the leg, just below the calf, with your thumbs to one side, fingers to the other. Squeeze into the muscles, forming a 'V' between your forefingers and thumbs. Squeeze up over the calf muscles, releasing the pressure as you near the knee.

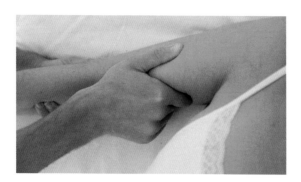

the upper arm Support the forearm and elbow. Position your other hand at the front of the arm, either side of the muscles above the elbow. Squeeze upward, pressing with your thumb, rolling the muscles between your thumb and forefinger. Work up the front of the arm several times.

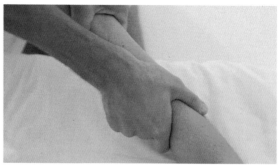

the forearms Support the arm at the wrist. Place your other hand over the forearm, thumb to the outside, fingers on the inside. Squeeze up the muscles toward the elbow, applying pressure between your forefinger and thumb. Repeat several times, easing the strokes at the elbow.

opening

Opening uses a spreading movement of the thumbs or pressure with the heels of the hands, helping to disperse tension after deeper releasing strokes. Opening strokes move out across the body rather than up or down. Opening can return the hands to a certain position on the body, or be interchanged with wringing, followed by softer strokes. Cup your hands right around the muscles to make opening most effective.

the thighs Place both hands over the front of the thigh, thumbs together in the centre, fingers cupped around the muscles. Press down and draw outward, using the heels of your hands to give firm pressure. Repeat the stroke up and down the thigh, easing pressure near the knee.

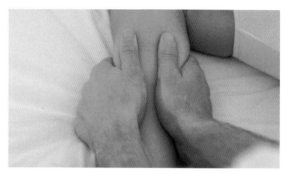

the arms Cup both hands around the upper arm and place your thumbs together in the centre, facing you and pointing upward. Apply pressure and draw the thumbs outward to the sides of the arm. Repeat the movement slightly further down and continue to the wrist.

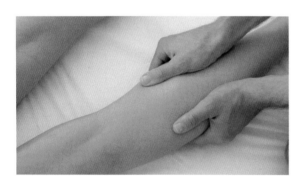

the calves Cup your hands around the top of the calf, thumbs lying lengthways in the centre. Draw the thumbs apart, spreading out across the muscles to the fingers. Work down the calf, releasing pressure at the bottom. Use the base of your thumbs to firmly squeeze the muscles.

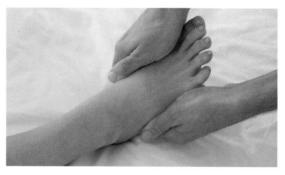

the foot Place your thumbs together over the top of the foot just below the ankle, fingertips curled underneath. Slide the thumbs toward the sides of the foot, stimulating and squeezing the muscles. Use the pads of your thumbs. Repeat once further down, without pressing the toes.

circling

Circling provides a soft, round movement over the body. The stroke can be used both for far-reaching release, as over the sacrum, or as a soothing, relaxing stroke, for example, over the abdomen. You can either circle with both hands, in alternate directions, singly, or with one hand placed on top of the other. Always keep your hands flat against the skin and very soft, even when you are circling over the bone. Circling can be used either to release or to gently diffuse the effects of kneading, and can often be used to replace pulling strokes up the body or to return the attention, and your hands, from one area to another. It also gives a sense of movement and expansion, such as circling over the ribs, and brings a pleasant sense of softness to the body massage and to your partner.

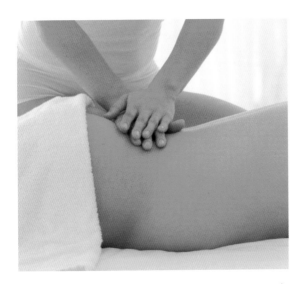

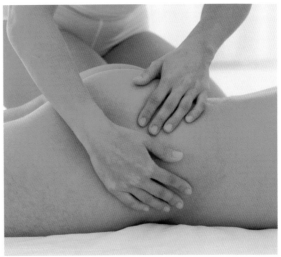

the lower back Place one hand on top of the other over the sacrum (the bony triangle at the base of the spine). Circle the hands in an anticlockwise direction over the sacrum and lower back, keeping the fingertips flat against the body. Keep your strokes precise and avoid straying from the centre of the back.

the buttocks Lean over your partner. Place one hand over the hip and circle in an anticlockwise direction, then circle with the other hand the opposite way. Keep your hands flat and the movements firm. Make broad circles over the hips and buttocks, alternating your hands so that your strokes flow continuously.

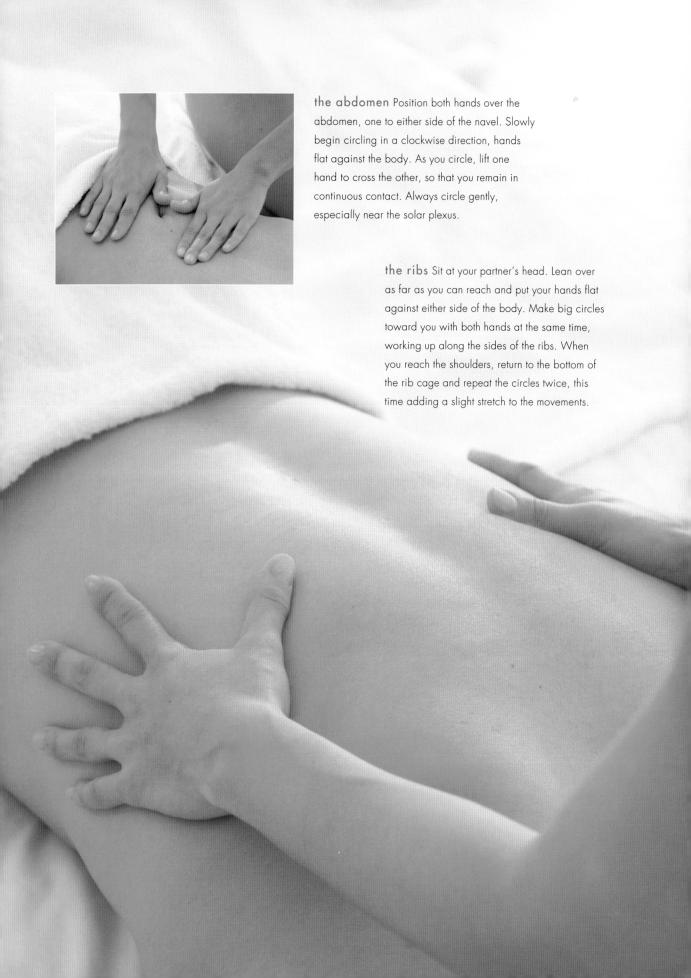

the abdomen Position both hands over the abdomen, one to either side of the navel. Slowly begin circling in a clockwise direction, hands flat against the body. As you circle, lift one hand to cross the other, so that you remain in continuous contact. Always circle gently, especially near the solar plexus.

the ribs Sit at your partner's head. Lean over as far as you can reach and put your hands flat against either side of the body. Make big circles toward you with both hands at the same time, working up along the sides of the ribs. When you reach the shoulders, return to the bottom of the rib cage and repeat the circles twice, this time adding a slight stretch to the movements.

feathering

In feathering you use the tips of the fingers to gently stroke down the body, alternating hands for a continuous rippling effect. It is one of the lightest, softest massage strokes and one of the most delightful! Feathering is used to conclude after you have massaged each section of the body, or it can be used as a final stroke bringing the massage to a close. Always stroke downward and finally lift the hands so your movements will end almost imperceptibly. Feathering not only feels good, it serves a purpose, drawing the mind and senses down the body, connecting one area to another, and it can be used to draw tension out through the fingers or toes. Don't even feel tempted to skip it.

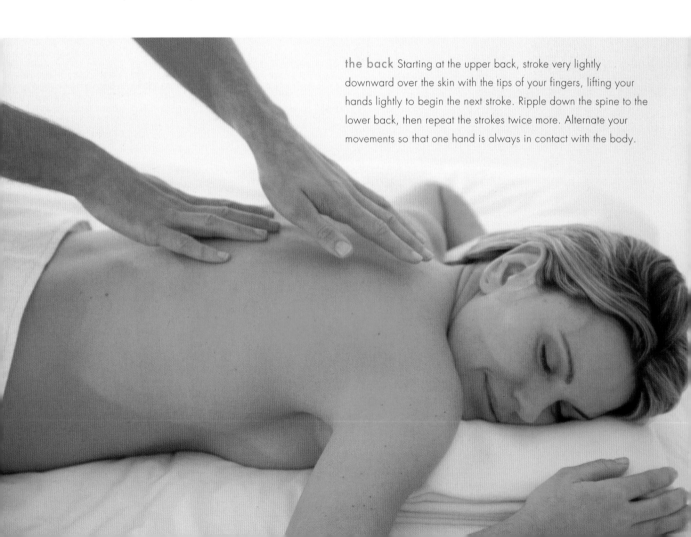

the back Starting at the upper back, stroke very lightly downward over the skin with the tips of your fingers, lifting your hands lightly to begin the next stroke. Ripple down the spine to the lower back, then repeat the strokes twice more. Alternate your movements so that one hand is always in contact with the body.

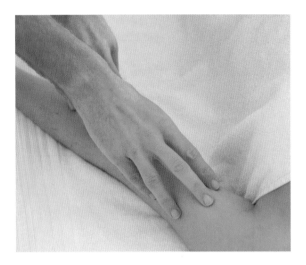

the arms Stroke with your fingers over the shoulder and then continue to feather lightly down the arm to the wrist. Alternate the hands, starting the movements a little further down the arm each time. Lift the fingers at the end of each stroke, rather like stroking a cat. End by feathering the tips of the fingers.

the legs Begin this movement at the top of the thigh. Feather lightly down the leg and over the knee to the calf. Stroke with the fingertips, moving your hands alternately in a flowing rhythm. Stroke over the front of the ankle then slowly off over the toes. This gives the feeling of connecting the whole leg.

the feet Support the foot with one hand and with the other feather in one movement from the heel to the toes. Repeat the soft stroking movements several times. Remember to stroke right over the tips of the toes and to continue the movement for a few seconds after. Firmer strokes will prevent tickling.

the hands Hold the hand, palm upward, and with your other hand stroke lightly from the wrist to the fingertips. Draw your hand very slowly off the fingers and as you do so, feel that you are drawing tension out through the body. These strokes can be very soft, following each other in waves.

pressing

Pressing is a stroke performed with the pads of the thumbs. The thumbs can press alternately (as over the palms), singly or one on top of the other (as over the forehead) where the body does not need to be supported. Pressing is used to release the muscles over a specific, usually small, area. The technique works best on soft, sensitive areas where you could not use kneading or squeezing, but are not too muscular so you can press over the bone. This type of thumb pressure aims at general tension release. You may cover pressure points, but this is not the main purpose of the strokes. The movements can either be slow and deep, or quicker to cover an area rapidly, and are usually used together with loosening strokes.

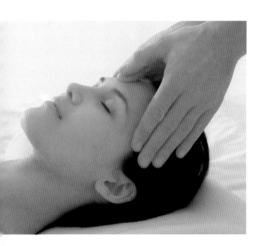

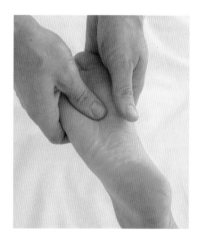

the forehead Resting your fingers at the side of the head, place one thumb over the other in the centre of the forehead. Beginning just above the eyebrows, press lightly with the thumbs and then release. Keep pressing up the forehead, each time starting a little further up, and continue to the hairline, then repeat.

the palms Support the hand from underneath with your fingers and place your thumbs over the top. Press down with the length of one thumb, release and repeat the movement with the other. Press alternately with the thumbs quite firmly over the palm, with most of the pressure coming from the pads.

the soles Support the foot with your fingers and place your thumbs over the sole. Press down with the length of one thumb, release, then press with the other, covering as much of the sole as you can. Include the heel, but be very gentle over the instep. Firm pressure avoids any accidental tickling.

raking

Raking is a wonderful stroke. By forming the hand into a claw-like shape, you then rake down or across the body, the hand shape allowing you to apply firm fingertip pressure. Unusually, the more angular your hands the better the movement works. Raking is rarely used on areas of the body other than the back, hips or tops of the thighs, where there is a lot of muscle. It is often used as the second half of a stroke, such as ironing or circling, over the spine and it releases tension down the back while at the same time returning the hands to the lower spine. Across the buttocks it can be used with pulling, after the deep releasing strokes. Be careful not to dig in too hard and follow with soft feathering as a contrast.

the upper back Form one hand into a claw by raising the wrist and angling the fingers. Position it at the top of the back, fingers spread to the sides of the spine. Interlace your other hand so the fingers also touch the back. Pressing with the fingertips, draw downward over the muscles.

the lower back Spread one hand, fingers to the sides of the spine, in the middle of the back. Raise your wrists, form a claw shape and press with the fingertips. Place your other hand a little further down and, starting with the lower hand, draw both hands down to the lower back. Lift away from the body lightly.

the hips Lean over your partner and place one hand just below the hip. Raise the wrist and rake back up toward you over the buttock and then begin the same movement with the other hand. Rake with the hands alternately. Continue the strokes over the buttock and hip, then rake over the top of the thigh.

stretching

Stretching is a beautiful addition to any body massage. Although working the muscles feels wonderful, the body can still feel compressed. Simple pulling or stretching affects the fibrous tissue around the joints and reduces muscle tension, leading to functional lengthening. Stretching gives a sense of expansion, taking the body beyond its functional limits and relaxing the muscles while restoring its range of movement. It should always be performed after the muscles have been warmed up and some of the tension released. The movements leading into each stretch need to be smooth, the muscles as relaxed as possible. Release the pull when you feel resistance and try again. Always stretch from a comfortable position.

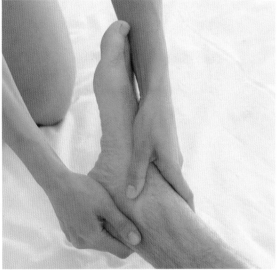

the neck Place your fingertips pointing downward over the top of the chest. Draw over the shoulders and under the neck in one movement, cupping the hands under the base of the skull. Holding firmly, but without pinching, pull directly back toward you, then release, for a stretch down the spine.

the legs Cup one hand under the heel of the foot, lifting the leg, and place the other hand over the top. Slowly pull back toward you, pulling mainly with the lower hand. Aim to get the movement coming from the hip. When you feel the joints resist, release and gently lower the leg, then try again.

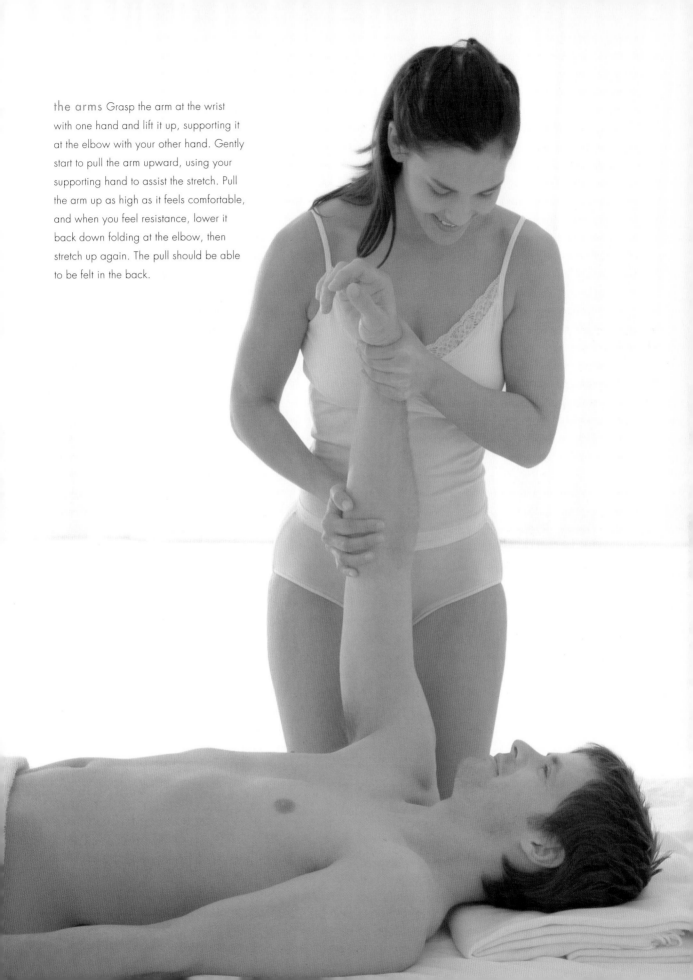

the arms Grasp the arm at the wrist with one hand and lift it up, supporting it at the elbow with your other hand. Gently start to pull the arm upward, using your supporting hand to assist the stretch. Pull the arm up as high as it feels comfortable, and when you feel resistance, lower it back down folding at the elbow, then stretch up again. The pull should be able to be felt in the back.

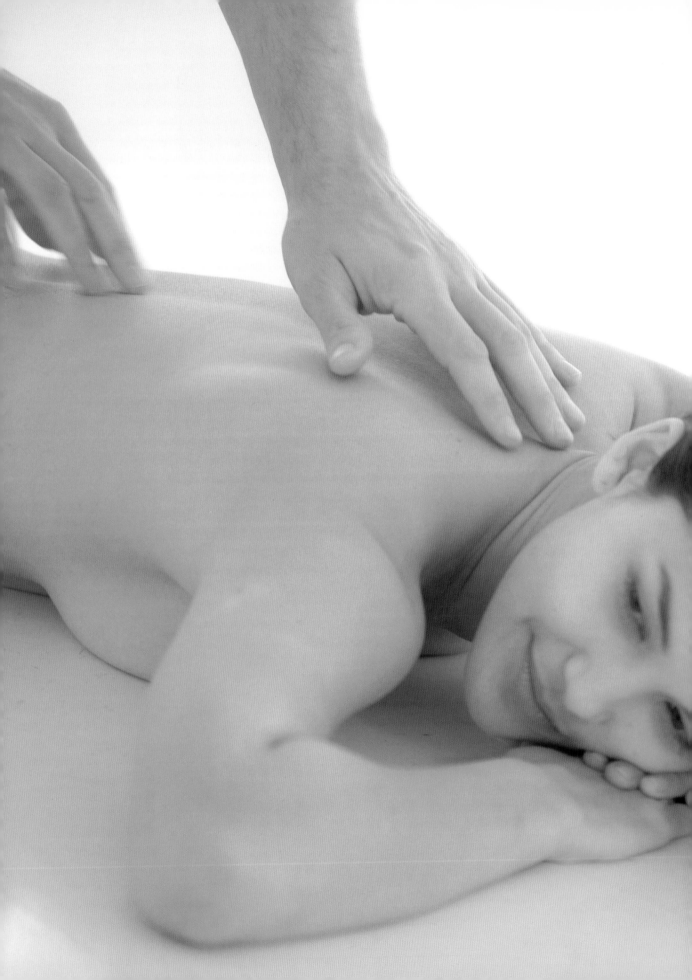

simple massage

The simple massage that follows is intended as a starting point, incorporating the techniques explained on the previous pages into a sequence that takes around 30 minutes. First master these simple movements, so that eventually you will be able to make up your own strokes and develop your own sequence and style. When you massage, always make sure you are in the correct position, with your back as straight as possible, and put your weight behind your strokes. While most people say they like firm pressure, err on the gentle side at first (you can always increase it) and check with your partner frequently. As long as you are sensitive to your partner's needs and health concerns beforehand, whatever you do is sure to be appreciated! The simple massage begins on the back and leads to enormous rewards from your very first touch.

the back

The back is the largest and most important area you will massage all at once and so the massage itself is divided into sections of the shoulders, lower back and spine. The back is a great opportunity to ease yourself into the massage, try out the techniques, and practise the long, sweeping strokes. Most people will feel comfortable about having their backs massaged and are able to relax easily. Giving a back massage feels immediately satisfying because of the breadth of the muscles and the fact you can actually see the difference you are making. As the back contains so many nerves and nerve endings, any massage you do here will have a direct and profound effect over your partner's entire body.

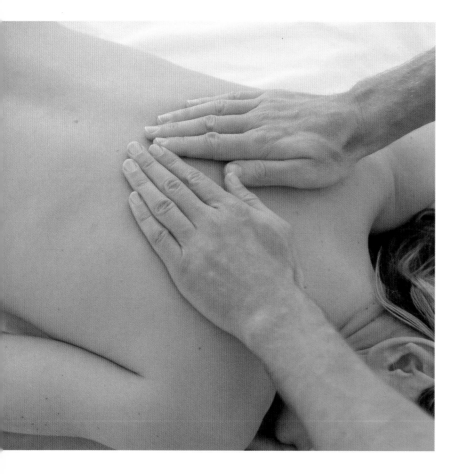

1 **effleurage** Begin the massage by positioning yourself at your partner's head. Rub a small amount of warmed oil between your hands. Place both hands together at the top of your partner's back and start to glide your hands downward. Keep your hands relaxed and flat against the back, both spreading the oil and feeling out your partner's muscles.

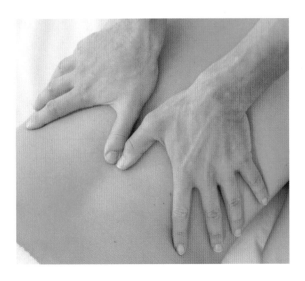

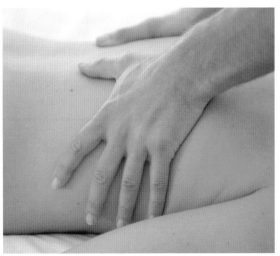

2 **effleurage** Glide to the lower back, separate your hands and sweep out around the hips. Then, start to draw your hands back up the body, this time stroking up the sides. Raise your wrists, to increase the contact of your fingers with your partner's body. Reduce your pressure slightly on the return stroke.

3 **effleurage** As you move right up the back, sweep your hands around the contours of your partner's shoulders, bringing your hands together again at the neck, and stroke lightly off the body. Repeat the whole stroke at least twice more, smoothing out your partner's muscles in preparation for the next stroke.

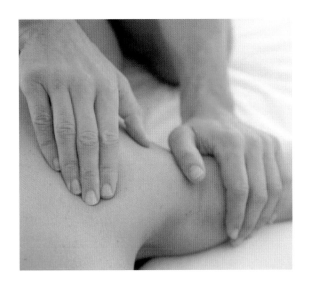

4 **easing the shoulder** Move to your partner's side. Support the shoulder gently with one hand and with the other, press, circle and squeeze around your partner's shoulder blade, using either your fingertips or the flat of your hand. This is a loosening and relaxing stroke, easing and softening the muscles.

5 **kneading the shoulder** Return to your partner's head. Begin to knead along the top of your partner's shoulder muscles, pushing in with your thumbs and rolling your fingers back toward you. Continue massaging along the shoulder to the neck. As this is a fairly compact area, your movements will naturally be quite small.

6 **shoulder push** In the same position, place the fingertips of both hands, one behind the other, at the inner edge of the shoulder blade. Now push both hands slowly downward, pressing firmly around the outline of the shoulder blade. Follow the contours with your hands, at the same time releasing any tension.

7 **shoulder pull** Continue the movement around the bottom of the shoulder blade, then separate your hands and draw them back up around the rest of the blade, keeping close in to the armpit. Your partner's shoulder should move as you pull. Repeat the whole stroke. This is excellent for loosening the shoulders.

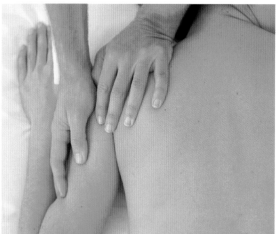

8 **pushing the shoulder down** After repeating the previous movement, end the sequence by placing both hands over your partner's shoulder and pushing the shoulder downward. The shoulder will move significantly, but only push as far as feels comfortable. Your partner will then feel a good release. Do the movement once only.

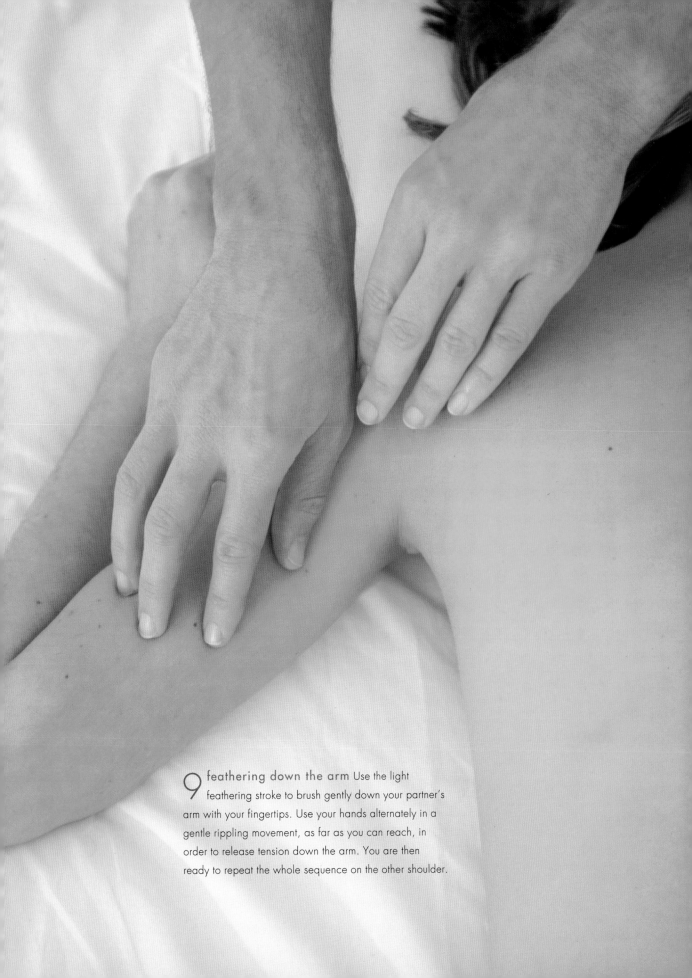

9 feathering down the arm Use the light
feathering stroke to brush gently down your partner's
arm with your fingertips. Use your hands alternately in a
gentle rippling movement, as far as you can reach, in
order to release tension down the arm. You are then
ready to repeat the whole sequence on the other shoulder.

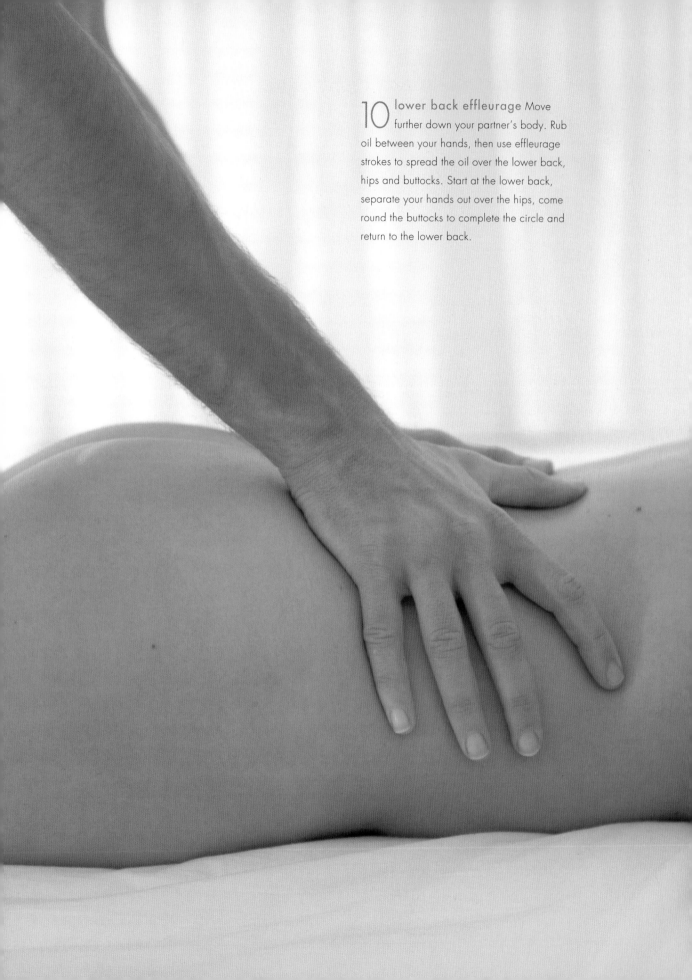

10 lower back effleurage Move
further down your partner's body. Rub
oil between your hands, then use effleurage
strokes to spread the oil over the lower back,
hips and buttocks. Start at the lower back,
separate your hands out over the hips, come
round the buttocks to complete the circle and
return to the lower back.

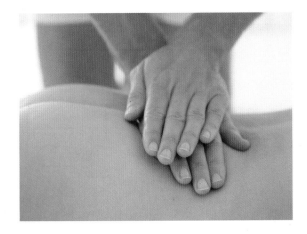

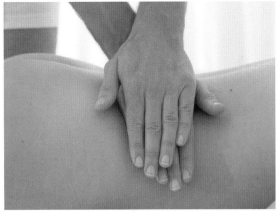

11 **circling the sacrum** Place one hand on top of the other, fingers flat, over your partner's sacrum (the bony triangle at the base of the spine). Slowly circle several times in an anticlockwise direction, using your upper hand for pressure. This is a wonderful tension release, but always check it feels comfortable for your partner.

12 **hip push** Place both hands, one on top of the other, in the centre of your partner's back. Start the stroke to the far side of the spine, just above the level of the hip. Now, push away from you, sliding your hands over the back and downward, but keeping your stroke above your partner's hips.

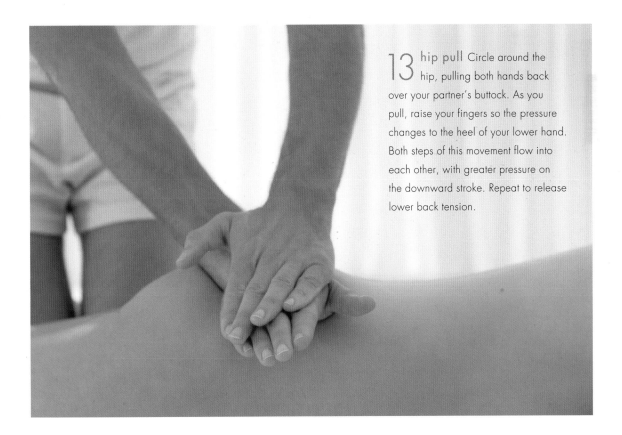

13 **hip pull** Circle around the hip, pulling both hands back over your partner's buttock. As you pull, raise your fingers so the pressure changes to the heel of your lower hand. Both steps of this movement flow into each other, with greater pressure on the downward stroke. Repeat to release lower back tension.

14 **kneading** Lean over your partner and begin kneading strokes on the buttock by pressing down into the flesh and away from you with your thumb, then rolling the muscles back toward you with your fingers. Move your hands in an alternating rhythm and work only on the soft muscles, avoiding the bone.

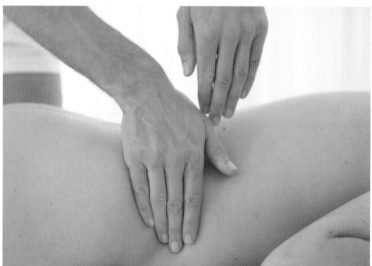

15 **pulling** Without breaking your movement, bring your hands just above your partner's hips. Slide one hand underneath the body, then bring your hand back toward you by pulling up your partner's side. Pull alternately with each hand, moving along the side of the body up toward the chest.

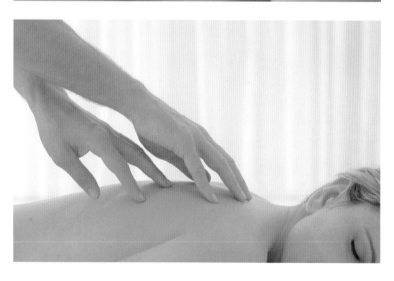

16 **feathering** When you reach the shoulder, use your fingertips alternately to softly feather the length of the back muscles, keeping to the far side of your partner's spine. Lift your hands away lightly at the end of each stroke. Repeat down the length of the spine several times, finishing at the lower back.

17 forearm stretch
Lean across to the far side of your partner's spine and rest both forearms together, facing each other, in the middle of your partner's back. Keep your wrists relaxed and your hands formed into loose fists. Using your body weight, start to apply pressure downward with your forearms.

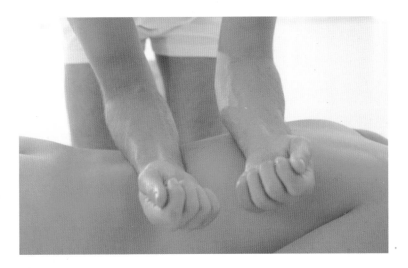

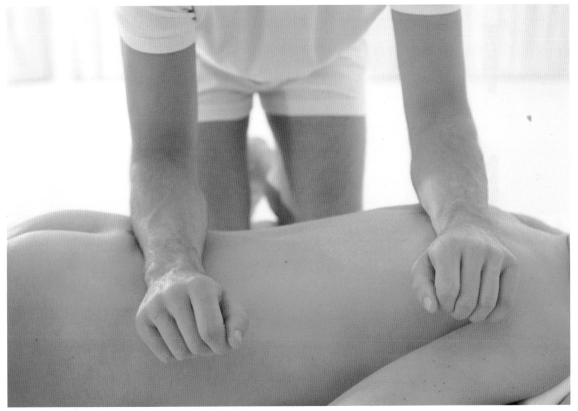

18 forearm stretch Now turn your forearms over and, still applying downward pressure, draw them slowly apart across your partner's back. Lean your weight into your arms and stretch until you reach the hip and shoulder. This not only feels great, but provides an excellent stretch for the muscles at the side of the spine. Repeat twice, change position and perform the lower back sequences on the other side.

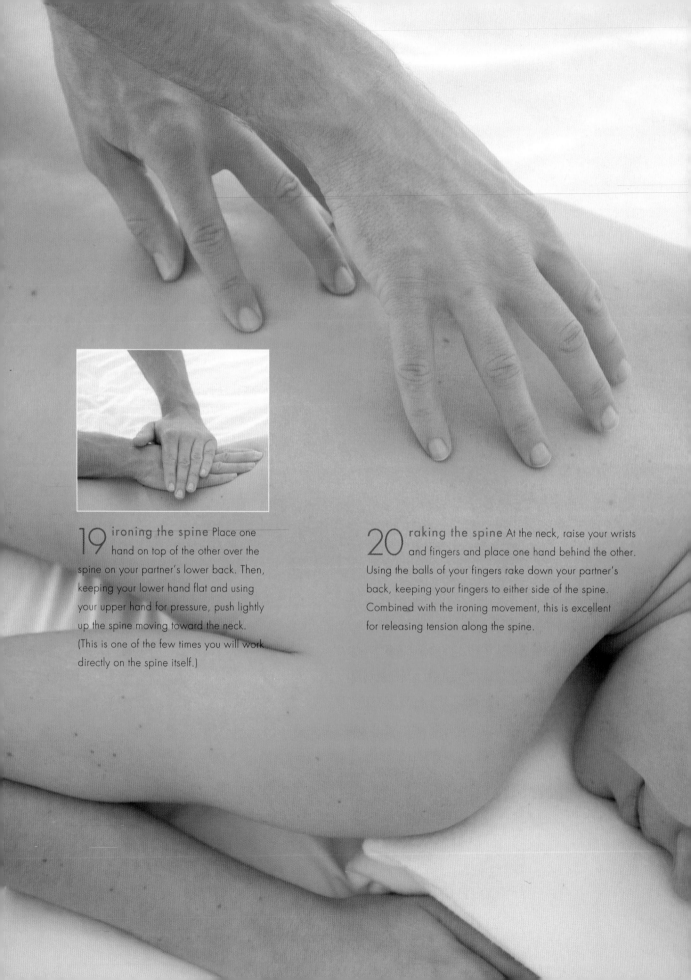

19 **ironing the spine** Place one hand on top of the other over the spine on your partner's lower back. Then, keeping your lower hand flat and using your upper hand for pressure, push lightly up the spine moving toward the neck. (This is one of the few times you will work directly on the spine itself.)

20 **raking the spine** At the neck, raise your wrists and fingers and place one hand behind the other. Using the balls of your fingers rake down your partner's back, keeping your fingers to either side of the spine. Combined with the ironing movement, this is excellent for releasing tension along the spine.

21 stroking the spine Return your hands to your partner's upper back and stroke lightly down the spine several times. This is a profoundly relaxing and soothing stroke, which gives the feeling of connecting the entire back. It is also a stroke for warming down and bringing the massage on the back toward its close.

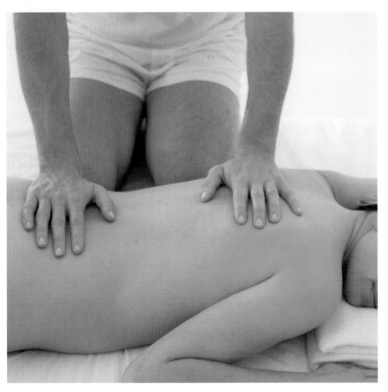

22 resting This movement is deceptive, for it is not as passive as it appears. To complete the back massage, place both hands on your partner's back. Feel the energy coming out through the palms of your hands, at the same time feeling your partner's back coming into balance. After all the work you have done, it is important to spend a few quiet moments for everything to settle before you move on.

the back of the legs

When you come to massage the legs you begin to feel a real sense of giving a full body massage. The legs offer you an opportunity to work on some of the body's most powerful muscles, and you can really get to grips with some of the basic strokes. While you should approach the legs as a whole, in reality your movements will be divided between the upper and lower legs and the feet. The secret of a fantastic leg massage is to adjust your strokes to the length of the muscles and not to taper off too soon. The leg stretch needs to be performed by you both confidently and comfortably, and gets better each time you practise. Once it becomes familiar, it will give the massage an added depth.

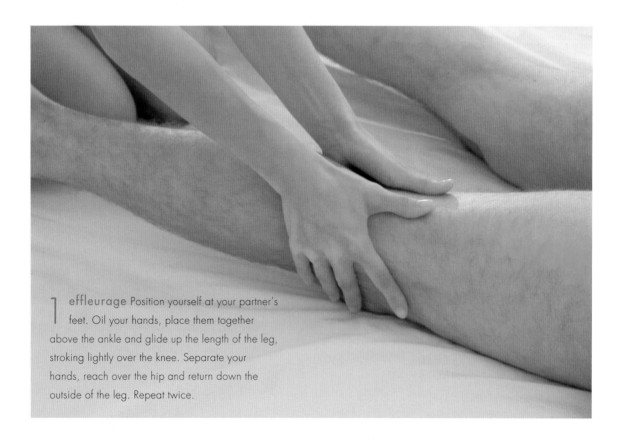

1 **effleurage** Position yourself at your partner's feet. Oil your hands, place them together above the ankle and glide up the length of the leg, stroking lightly over the knee. Separate your hands, reach over the hip and return down the outside of the leg. Repeat twice.

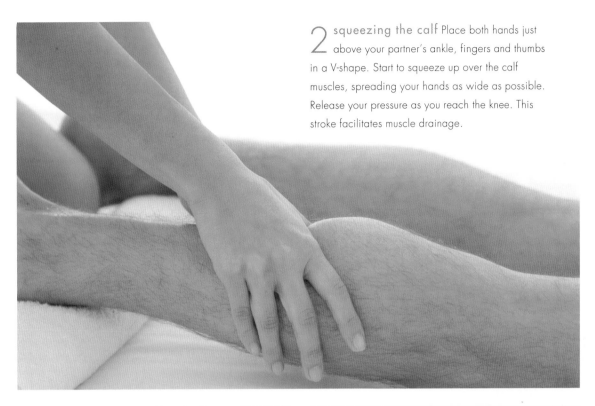

2 **squeezing the calf** Place both hands just above your partner's ankle, fingers and thumbs in a V-shape. Start to squeeze up over the calf muscles, spreading your hands as wide as possible. Release your pressure as you reach the knee. This stroke facilitates muscle drainage.

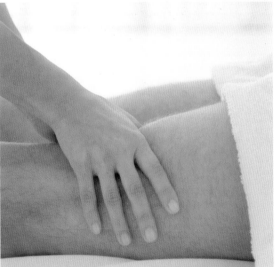

3 **squeezing the thigh** Brush the back of the knee lightly, then resume the squeezing movement up the back and outer thigh, keeping pressure away from the inner thigh. Continue up to the hip, putting your full body weight behind the movement to achieve a good, firm pressure.

4 **kneading the thigh** Change your position so you are square-on to your partner. Slowly start to knead the muscles over the back of the thigh. You can afford to use a firm pressure here, but check this as you are working. You will find the muscles move quite easily as you massage.

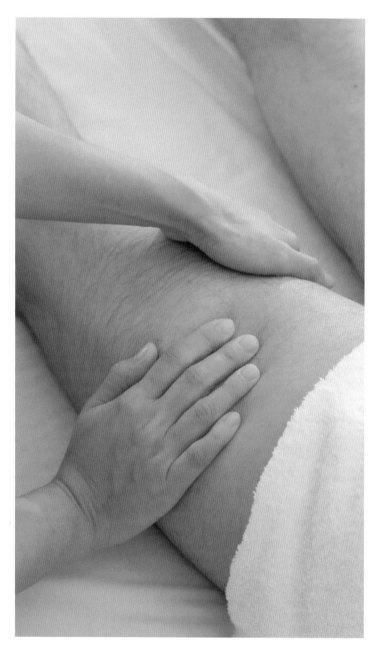

6 **stretching the leg** Move to your
partner's foot. Place one hand
underneath the ankle for support and your
other hand around the heel. Now, use
your body weight to lean backward and
pull the length of your partner's leg. You
should be able to see this movement at the
hip. The direction of the pull needs to be
backward, rather than upward, and will
give the leg a wonderful stretch.

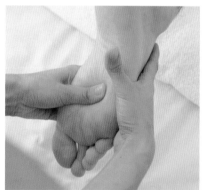

5 **wringing the thigh** Place one hand over your partner's outer thigh,
the other hand resting on the inside. Start to slide your hands toward
each other, pressing the muscles firmly so they twist as your hands cross.
Bring your hands to opposite sides of the thigh. Repeat the stroke the other
way, working down to the knee.

7 **pressing the foot** Gently lower
the leg and cup your hands around
your partner's foot. With the balls of your
thumbs, press right over the sole of the
foot, covering it several times. You can
use firm pressure, especially if your
partner is ticklish, but avoid pressing
over the instep.

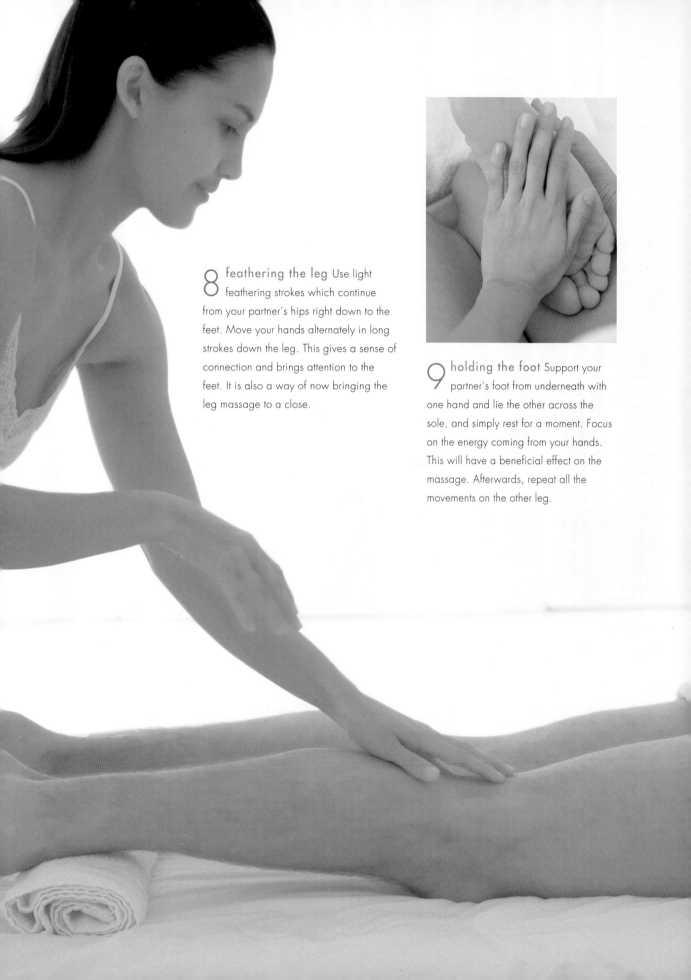

8 **feathering the leg** Use light feathering strokes which continue from your partner's hips right down to the feet. Move your hands alternately in long strokes down the leg. This gives a sense of connection and brings attention to the feet. It is also a way of now bringing the leg massage to a close.

9 **holding the foot** Support your partner's foot from underneath with one hand and lie the other across the sole, and simply rest for a moment. Focus on the energy coming from your hands. This will have a beneficial effect on the massage. Afterwards, repeat all the movements on the other leg.

the neck

Front of the body massage begins at your partner's neck and is effectively a continuation of the back massage. In fact, the two areas should be seen as one, but it is easier and more effective to massage the neck in this position. As the neck can be particularly sensitive to touch, you will need to approach it carefully. Shown here are some simple but effective movements. The neck stretch feels absolutely wonderful and will make your partner feel at least two inches taller. Your partner should be encouraged to relax and simply let you do the strokes without tensing up or helping in any way. Try to keep your movements flowing and confident so your partner will let go and have total trust in your hands.

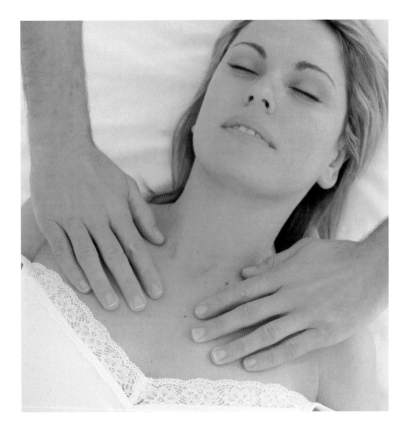

1 **neck stretch** Sit at your partner's head and rub a very little oil between your hands. Place them, fingers pointing downward, at the top of your partner's chest. Keeping your hands in full contact with your partner's body, draw them outward over the shoulders and slide round underneath the neck.

2 **neck stretch** Fingers facing upward beneath the neck, bring your hands back toward you until they are cupped around the base of your partner's skull and gently pull. The direction of the pull should be back toward you, rather than up. Only do this once. The two steps should feel like one movement.

3 **rolling the neck** Now place both hands under your partner's neck. Start to draw one hand up the muscles at the side of the neck, rolling the head in the opposite direction. Then roll the neck the other way with your other hand, so the head turns back again. Roll the neck back and forth between your hands several times. Encourage your partner to relax during the strokes in order to feel the full benefit of the movements.

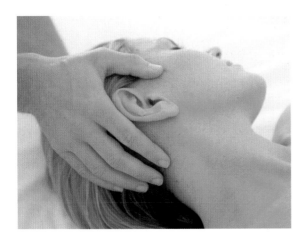

4 **turning the head** In order to perform the next movement, you will need to turn your partner's head. To do this smoothly, place both hands at the side of the head, thumbs in front of the ears, hands cupping the skull. Turn the head so that it rests on one hand, leaving your upper hand free to massage.

5 **shampooing the scalp** With the head resting on your lower hand, use your free hand to make shampooing movements over your partner's scalp. You can use quite firm pressure, as this usually feels fantastic. Cover the half of the scalp you can reach using the balls of your fingers, then turn the head to repeat the shampooing movements on the other side of your partner's scalp.

the face

Having your face massaged feels blissful. A gentle face massage has a positive effect over the whole body and can really act as an aid to deep relaxation. Men and women alike can appreciate the sensation of the face muscles relaxing, particularly around the forehead and jaw. Keep your movements as delicate and precise as possible, making sure you don't lean any weight on your partner, and try to avoid accidentally brushing the eyes, eyelashes or nostrils. Always be very sensitive. You can use either a very little or no oil, but be careful not to stretch or pull the skin as you work. Make sure your movements always end in an upward direction, in order that your partner is left with a positive feeling.

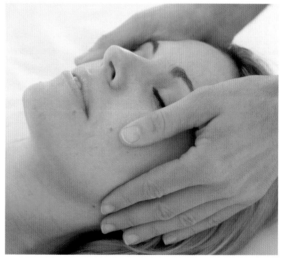

1 **drawing across the forehead** Cup your hands gently around your partner's head, without applying any pressure. Now place the length of your thumbs together in the centre of the forehead, just above the eyebrows. Keeping your thumbs flat, slowly draw them apart until you reach the hairline. Have in mind the idea of dispersing any tension. Repeat this movement several times.

2 **drawing under the cheeks** Resting your fingers at the side of your partner's face, place the balls of your thumbs beside the nostrils, just below the cheekbones. Once more, draw your thumbs apart following under the line of the cheekbones. Continue the movement toward the ears, ending with an upward stroke. Do this once.

3 **drawing under the chin** Place your hands in the centre of your partner's chin. Your thumbs should be just above the chin, your fingers just below. Now slide your hands out along the jaw line, squeezing gently between your thumbs and fingers. Follow round as far as you can, stroking upward toward the ears.

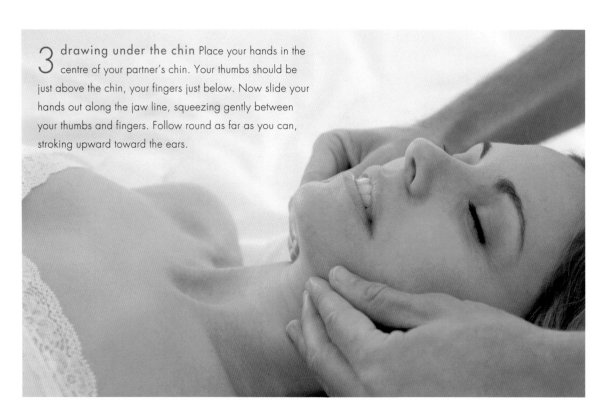

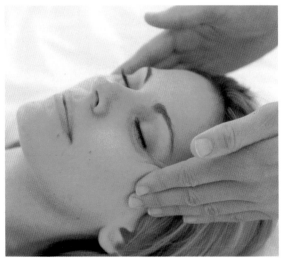

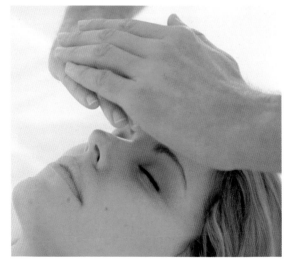

4 **circling the jaw** Place the pads of your fingers to either side of your partner's jaw, just below the cheekbones. (If you open and close your own mouth, you will feel the places where the muscles work.) Start to circle over the muscles very slowly for an effective release of tension. Make the circles quite large, keeping your fingers together.

5 **resting** To complete the face massage, place your hands gently over, but not touching, your partner's eyes. Again, think of the energy coming through your hands. Hold your hands in this position for a few moments. As well as relaxing your partner, this movement both rests and revitalizes the eyes.

the arms

The massage on the arms is similar in approach to the massage on the legs. While the arms should be regarded as a whole, you will find that your massage strokes naturally divide between your partner's upper arms, forearms and hands. The arm stretch provides an opportunity to work on the shoulder and back. As with the leg massage, the key to a successful arm massage is to follow all the muscles from beginning to end. Your partner should be encouraged to totally relax and not try to hold on or help. As the muscles are more difficult to reach with the arm lying flat, support it for most of the movements. The muscles may look delicate, but you will find that you can keep your pressure quite firm.

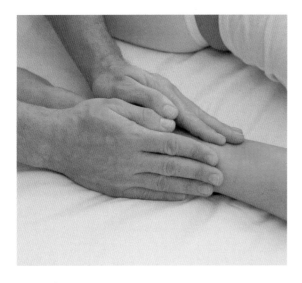

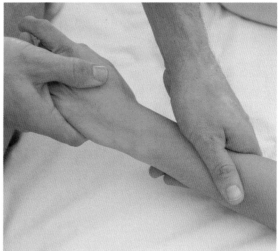

1 **effleurage** Move to your partner's side. Rub some oil onto your hands and then, beginning at the wrist, use effleurage strokes to spread the oil up over your partner's arm. Use greater pressure on the upward stroke, sweep over the shoulder and return to the wrist. Repeat this stroke twice more.

2 **squeezing the forearm** Supporting your partner's arm with one hand, place the other over the forearm, thumb on top and fingers underneath. Beginning at the wrist, squeeze up along the length of the muscles, tapering off as you near the elbow. This stimulates the muscles and releases tension. Repeat this movement several times.

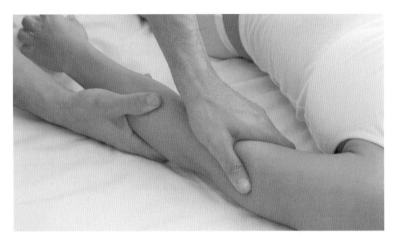

3 upper arm squeezing

Supporting your partner's upper arm, continue the squeezing movements between the thumb and the fingers. Start by beginning just above the elbow and squeeze up the muscles to the top of the arm, reaching as far as you can. Apply most of your pressure to the front of the arm and repeat several times.

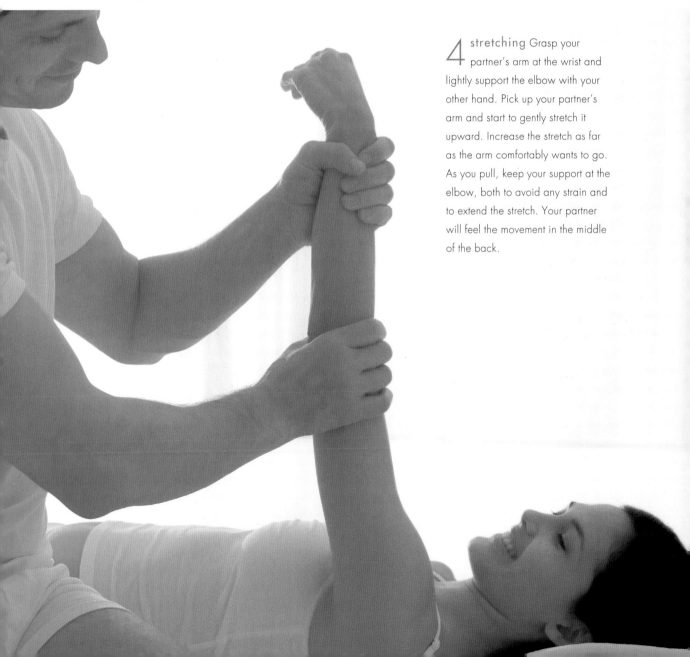

4 stretching

Grasp your partner's arm at the wrist and lightly support the elbow with your other hand. Pick up your partner's arm and start to gently stretch it upward. Increase the stretch as far as the arm comfortably wants to go. As you pull, keep your support at the elbow, both to avoid any strain and to extend the stretch. Your partner will feel the movement in the middle of the back.

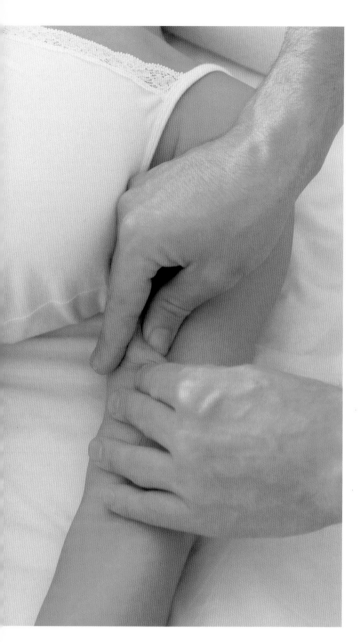

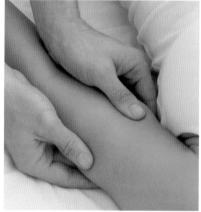

6 **opening the arm** Place both hands around your partner's upper arm, thumbs together at the front, fingers cupped around the back. Slowly draw both thumbs apart, applying pressure with the base. Repeat the movement slightly further down the arm and continue down the forearm to the wrist.

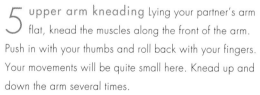

5 **upper arm kneading** Lying your partner's arm flat, knead the muscles along the front of the arm. Push in with your thumbs and roll back with your fingers. Your movements will be quite small here. Knead up and down the arm several times.

7 **opening the hand** Place your hands in the same position over your partner's hand and again draw the length of your thumbs apart. Keep your movement over the back of the hand, the pressure well above your partner's fingers. The hand will arch as you do this stroke, which has an excellent releasing effect.

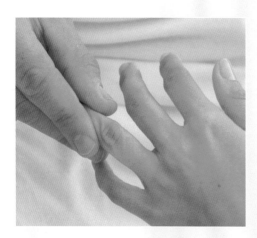

8 **twisting the fingers** Put your thumb and forefinger around the base of your partner's finger and twist down the sides of the finger to the tip. You can do this stroke quite firmly. Twist down each finger of the hand in turn, including the thumb, loosening up the fingers as you do so.

9 **pulling the fingers** Hold one of your partner's fingers between your own, your forefinger over the base of the finger, thumb underneath. Slowly pull the length of the finger, coming off at the tip. Squeeze gently as you pull to draw out any tension. Repeat the movement on each finger in turn, then change your position to perform the entire sequence on the other arm.

the chest

This massage affords you the opportunity to clear tension in the upper chest, the cause of which is particularly connected to the effects of stress. If you are massaging a woman keep your strokes either in the centre of the chest between the breasts or around the side of the ribs, but never massage the breasts directly. If you are at all nervous about this, keep your movements clear and confident, be very sure about the purpose of your strokes and then your partner will be able to relax as well. The shape of the ribs is great for strokes using the whole hand and for moulding your movements around the body. Pushing the shoulders reinforces the sense of lengthening and promotes total relaxation.

1 **effleurage** Move to your partner's head. Rub some oil between your hands and place them together at the top of your partner's chest. With your fingers pointing downward, glide your hands down the centre of the chest to the bottom of the rib cage, using the tips and length of your fingers.

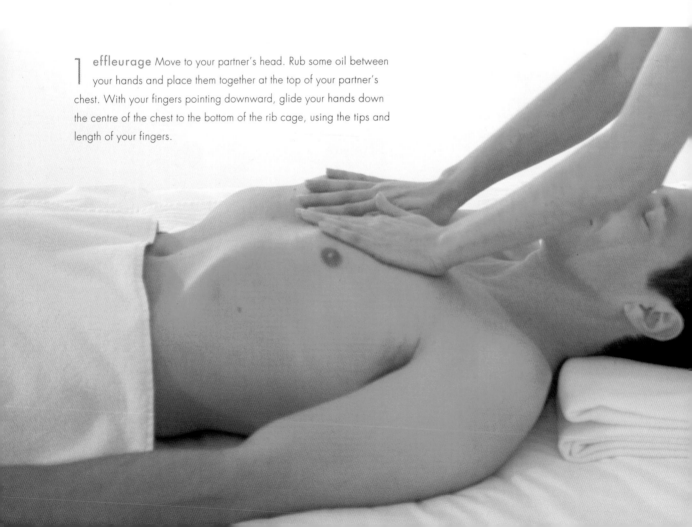

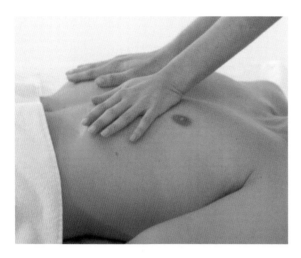

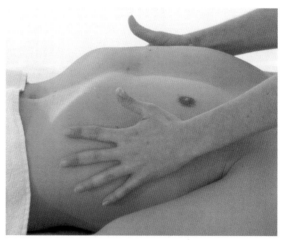

2 **pulling up** At the bottom of the ribs spread your hands, fingers pointing outward along the ribs, then draw them together and come back up the centre of the chest to your starting position. Use lighter pressure on your return stroke and finish using the tips of your fingers.

3 **pulling up** Repeat the effleurage stroke down the centre of your partner's chest, but this time spread your hands right around the ribs and pull up the sides of your partner's body. Keep your hands flat against the ribs, fingers spread, pulling very slightly as you return back to the top of the chest.

4 **pushing down the shoulders** As you return from the upward stroke, bring your hands to the top of your partner's shoulders. Placing both hands firmly over the shoulders, push downward using the palms of your hands. Push the shoulders gently down as far as feels comfortable – you will be surprised how far they move. This will give your partner a great sensation of lengthening.

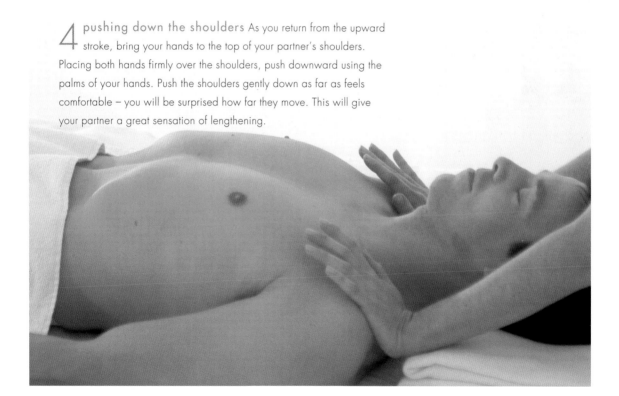

the abdomen

Massaging the abdomen is a special part of any body massage. We are all vulnerable and soft here, so whatever strokes you apply will penetrate deeply. The key is to be gentle and sensitive, and of all parts of the body massage, to think positively. Include the abdomen in any massage as relaxation here has a direct effect on the muscles. Over the abdomen you can use soft, circular movements using the flat of your hands. Move clockwise in order to follow the direction of the large intestine. The abdomen picks up stress quickly, so any soothing strokes will help. Be sensitive to your partner's menstrual cycle. It is fine to massage during menstruation, but check that she is not too sensitive to be touched.

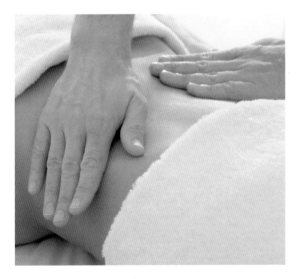

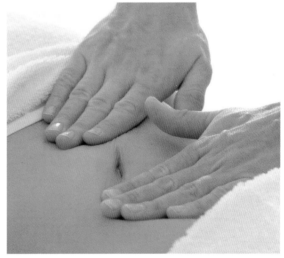

1 effleurage Sit at your partner's side. Rub some oil between your hands, spreading it over your partner's abdomen using soft, slow effleurage strokes. Always make sure your hands move in a clockwise direction. Use the whole of the hands, keeping them flat, and ensure your movements are sensitive to help your partner relax.

2 circling With one hand begin circling a little more firmly over the abdomen, still moving in a clockwise direction. Make your circle wide, taking in as large an area as possible within the boundary of the hips and rib cage. As one hand moves round, gently start to circle with your other hand.

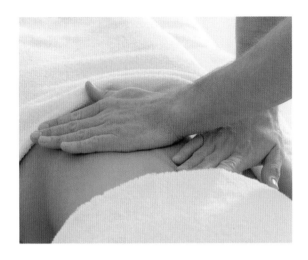

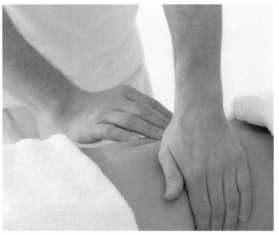

3 circling As your hands continue the circle they will naturally cross over each other. Make sure you always keep one hand in continuous contact with the abdomen and lift the other off as it crosses. This gives your partner a sense of continuity. Circle with soft, flat hands several times.

4 pulling Leaning over, place one hand underneath your partner's body, just above the hip. Pull your hand back up your partner's side toward you. Pull with each hand alternately, using a reasonable pressure so the body moves as you do. Repeat this several times on both sides, changing position if necessary.

5 resting Place both hands flat over your partner's abdomen and simply rest. As you do so, feel the energy coming out through your hands and keep your thoughts positive. Make sure you do not lean any weight on your partner. This movement feels extremely powerful and will balance your partner's energy.

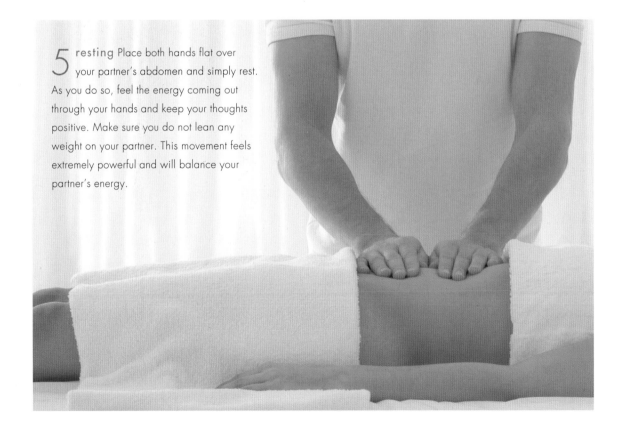

the front of the legs

This final part of the simple massage offers you an opportunity to work again on the legs and feet. You will now have covered all the accessible parts of your partner's body from head to toe. The fronts of the thighs contain powerful muscles, so even though you are bringing the massage to a close, your partner will miss out if you hurry. It is important to make sure your strokes cover the entire length of the legs and especially go right over the hip. Every second you spend working the muscles thoroughly will be appreciated deeply, together with what is often sadness that the massage is ending! Make sure that you give time to the ending. It is as important as the way you begin.

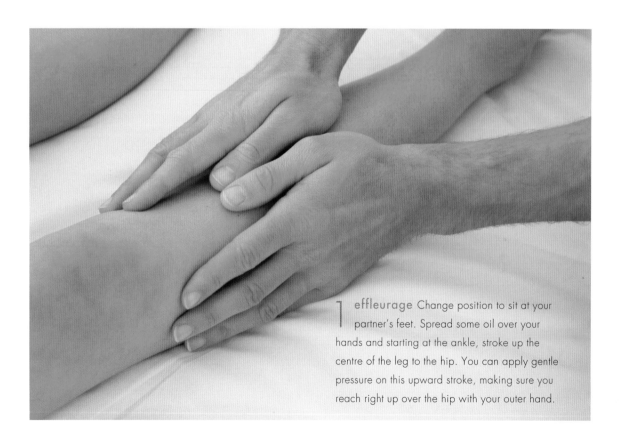

1 **effleurage** Change position to sit at your partner's feet. Spread some oil over your hands and starting at the ankle, stroke up the centre of the leg to the hip. You can apply gentle pressure on this upward stroke, making sure you reach right up over the hip with your outer hand.

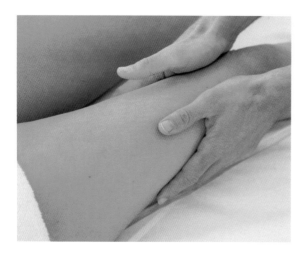

2 **effleurage** Now bring your hands back down the outside of your partner's leg to complete the effleurage stroke. Keep your pressure light and draw back down the leg, raising your wrists so that you are using your fingertips. When you reach the foot, repeat the stroke twice more.

3 **squeezing the calf** Place your hands over the front of your partner's leg, just above the ankle. Have your thumbs to one side, your fingers to the other. Start to squeeze up the calf muscles, pressing with your fingers and thumbs. Do not apply direct pressure to the shin and ease the movement as you near the knee.

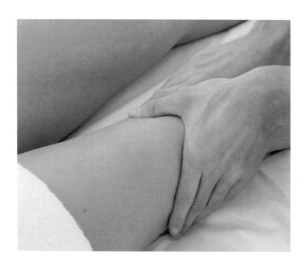

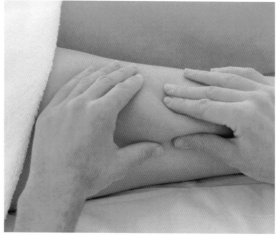

4 **squeezing the thigh** Change position so that you can reach your partner's thigh and continue the squeezing movements above the knee, your thumbs and fingers on either side of the leg. Squeeze as far as you can up the thigh, then round the movement off over the hip. Repeat the stroke as often as you need to.

5 **kneading the thigh** Begin kneading over your partner's thigh, feeling for any tension in the muscles and working your way back down again until you reach just above the knee. Work your way over the front and outer thigh, keeping pressure away from the inside thigh. Sit square-on to your partner and roll the muscles with your fingers and thumbs, pressing the flesh in and then rolling it back toward you.

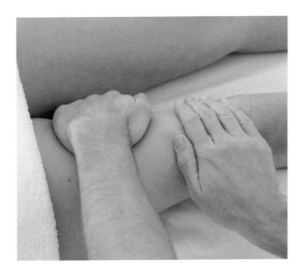

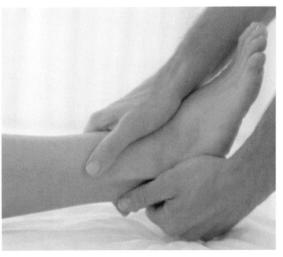

6 **wringing the thigh** Next, start wringing from the top of the thigh down your partner's leg. Placing both hands on opposite sides of the thigh, use a fairly firm pressure to bring your far hand back over the top of the leg toward you, your near hand pushing away from you. This produces a twist over the muscles.

7 **stretching the leg** Move to your partner's feet. Place one hand underneath the heel and the other over the top of the foot. Lift the leg slightly and pull slowly back toward you. This should be a comfortable stretch for your partner. The pull comes from your lower hand, your upper one is mainly supporting.

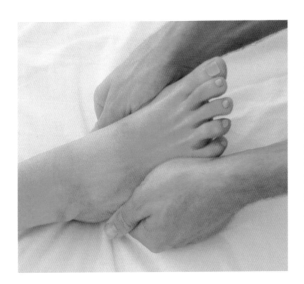

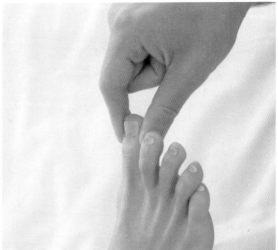

8 **opening the foot** Cup your fingers underneath your partner's foot, placing the length of your thumbs together over the top. Draw your hands apart to the sides of the foot, pressing mainly with the base of your thumbs. You can do this movement several times, keeping your pressure above the toes.

9 **pulling the toes** Take hold of your partner's toe between your thumb and forefinger. Gently wriggle up the side of the toe toward you, pulling as you continue off at the end. Slowly pull each toe in turn, keeping your pressure firm if your partner is ticklish. This movement will feel truly delightful.

10 **resting** Wrap your hands softly around your partner's foot and just hold for a moment. Feel the energy coming through your hands. Make this ending soft but definite, before repeating the same sequence on the other leg.

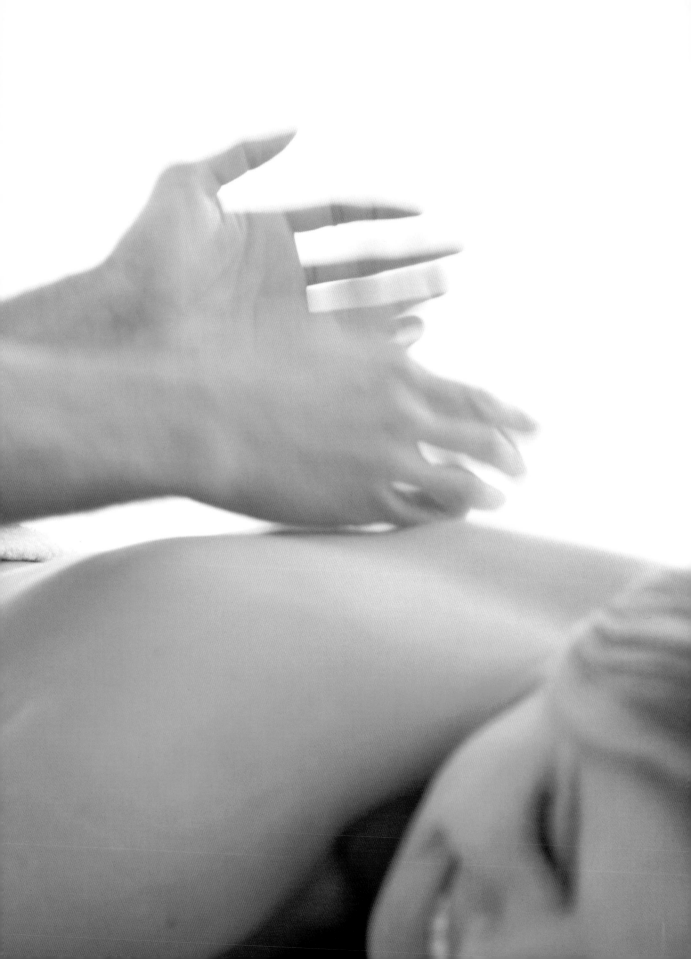

further techniques

The techniques included in the following section broaden your range and build upon those you have already learned. They require a greater familiarity with the body, the practice of massage and greater precision. They also ask for increased sensitivity. Again, the best way of getting to know the strokes is to try them out, experiment on different parts of the body and get lots of feedback. Also have your partner apply them to you, which is actually the best way to learn. The techniques can then be added to the strokes you already know and used to work on specific areas or problems. As always, pay attention to your own body as you massage, in particular the position of your back.

thumb rolling

Thumb rolling uses the length of the thumbs, pressing with the pads and the sides. Resting the fingers lightly on the body or holding your hands slightly away, roll the thumbs alternately so that the strokes follow on from each other, creating a wave of movement. Rolling is used to cover a specific area, such as the feet, or to follow the length of a band of muscle, such as along the side of the spine. It is used after firm, loosening strokes, to release and disperse tension, or to connect one area of the body to another, such as the upper and lower back. It is usually performed away from the centre of the body, or to roll from base to tip, for example, over the nose. It is followed by soft, soothing strokes.

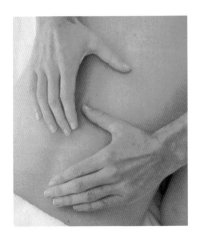

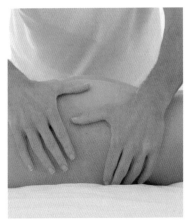

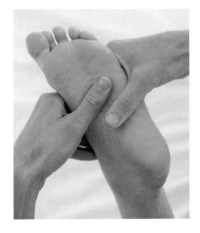

the spine Starting at the upper back, place the length of one thumb over the band of muscle to the side of the spine. Now roll downward, pushing the muscles away from you. Lift the thumb lightly and continue rolling with the other thumb, beginning slightly further down each time. Continue down the back.

the buttocks Position yourself at your partner's side. Lean over your partner and roll with one thumb diagonally across the buttock. Begin to the side of the sacrum (the bony triangle at the base of the spine) and work over toward the hip. Roll alternately with the thumbs, keeping the rolls quite short. Repeat the strokes from the beginning several times.

the soles of the feet Position yourself at your partner's feet. Support the foot from underneath with your fingers and place your thumbs over the sole. Roll the length of one thumb from the heel toward the toes, then roll in the same direction with the other thumb. Cover as much of the foot as you can. Be gentle over the instep and continue the stroke right to the toes.

thumb circling

For thumb circling, use the pads of the thumbs. The circling can either be
done on the spot, with the thumbs circling alternately, or the movement can
travel, with both thumbs circling over or around an area. In both cases, press
in and slowly circle with the pad of the thumb. Circling is done over soft, rather
than thick areas of muscle, where you will press down over bone (such as the
hands and feet), alongside the spine or around the joints (such as the wrists).
It can be used to release tension over small, specific areas of muscle or in a
more general sense to disperse tension after releasing work has been done.
Circling can also be used to great effect to release over and around the joints.

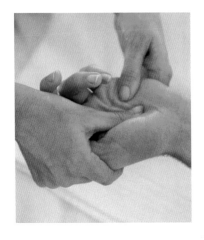

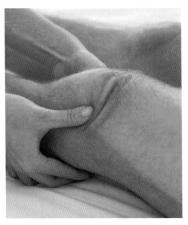

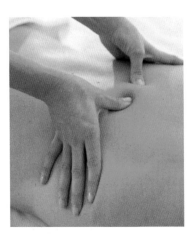

the palms Support the hand with
your fingers. Place the pad of your
thumb over the palm, press in and
circle outward. Then, circle outward
with the other thumb. Work over
the entire palm using both thumbs
alternately, making your circles fairly
large. Include the base of the fingers
and the heel of the hand.

the knees Position yourself at
your partner's feet. Support the knee
from underneath. Place both thumbs
at the base of the kneecap and
simultaneously circle outward. As
you circle move slightly further round
the kneecap, continuing the circling
movement until the thumbs meet
together at the top. Keep close in
as you circle, pressing in toward
the knee.

the spine Position yourself so
you can reach the length of your
partner's spine. Start at the lower
back, placing both thumbs on the
bands of muscle at the side of the
spine. Circle your thumbs outward
and as you do so travel up the spine.
Continue circling all the way up the
spine, stroking the muscles upward
and outward. Concentrate on any
tight spots you may feel.

friction

Friction is another type of circling, this time done with the pads and tips of the fingers or thumbs. Friction is a deep pressure stroke. The tight circling movement is performed while pressing into a specific spot, without moving over the skin, as a way of applying more pressure. The movement is very precise and is applied over a particularly tight area of muscle, such as at the side of the spine, or into or around a joint. The pressure needs to be adjusted to the area you are working on and can be quite gentle where necessary. Friction is an effective method of release, but is only to be applied sparingly to areas where deep release would be beneficial. In addition to the circling, a gentle vibration may be used.

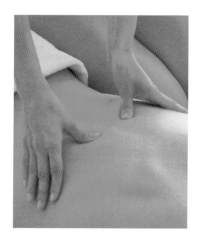

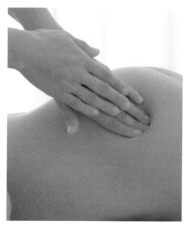

the spine Place both thumbs on the muscles to the side of the spine where you feel a particular tightness. Apply pressure downward into the muscles and as you do so, make a slight circling movement on the spot, without releasing the pressure. Continue for a few moments, checking the pressure with your partner, then release. This will help the muscles directly beneath your thumbs to relax.

the hip Place the tips of your fingers over the hip joint and then press diagonally in toward the joint. For deeper penetration circle on the spot with your fingers as you press. (As it is so deep you will not be able to reach the actual joint itself.) This movement helps to decrease any tension which may be held in the surrounding soft tissue.

the ankle Position yourself at your partner's feet. With one hand supporting the foot, use the thumb of the other to press all the way around the ankle joint. Use the pad of your thumb to press diagonally in toward the joint, again circling lightly as you do so. Check the pressure with your partner. Work all the way around the inside and outside of the ankle, keeping the pressure close into the joint.

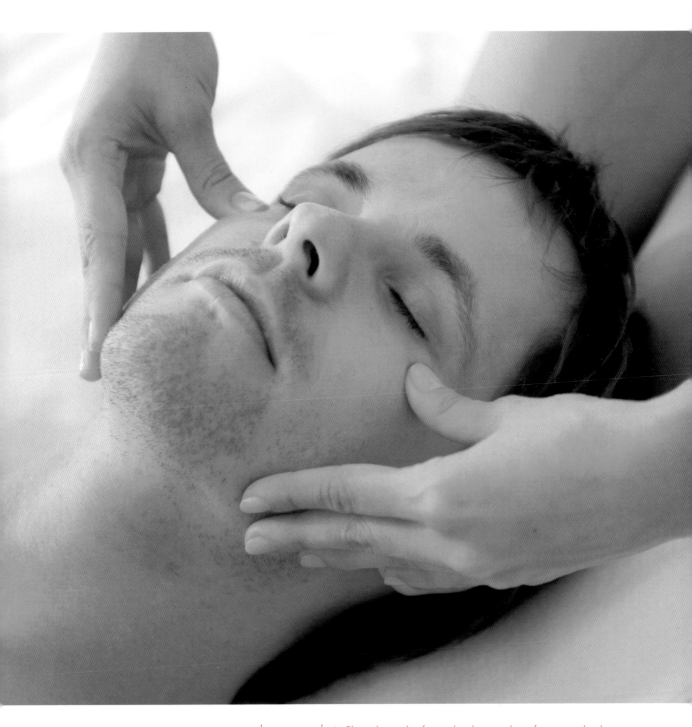

the eye sockets Place the pads of your thumbs over the soft tissue under the eye sockets. Using a light pressure, make minute circling movements, pressing inward. You can use a slight vibration at the same time. Work along under the eye socket toward the nose, keeping the movements small and precise. Avoid pressing the delicate tissue under the eye itself.

heel pressure

Using the heels of the hands is a way of increasing pressure over large or tight areas of muscle. Instead of using the fingers, the wrists are tilted back and pressure is applied with the heels of the hands, enabling you to use more of your body weight. The heels can enhance squeezing movements or be used for extra pressure on a specific area, for example the buttocks. The use of the heels allows for deeper penetration, particularly if the stroke is moving over the muscles. On the limbs, the strokes are always applied as you move toward the centre of the body and never on the downward stroke. As you apply pressure squeeze into the muscles, remembering to ease the strokes as you approach the joints.

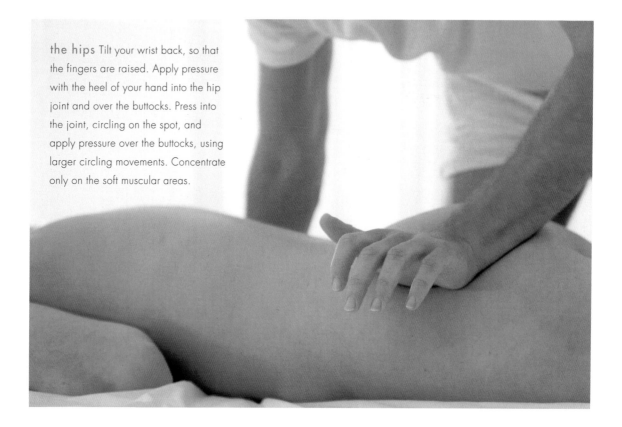

the hips Tilt your wrist back, so that the fingers are raised. Apply pressure with the heel of your hand into the hip joint and over the buttocks. Press into the joint, circling on the spot, and apply pressure over the buttocks, using larger circling movements. Concentrate only on the soft muscular areas.

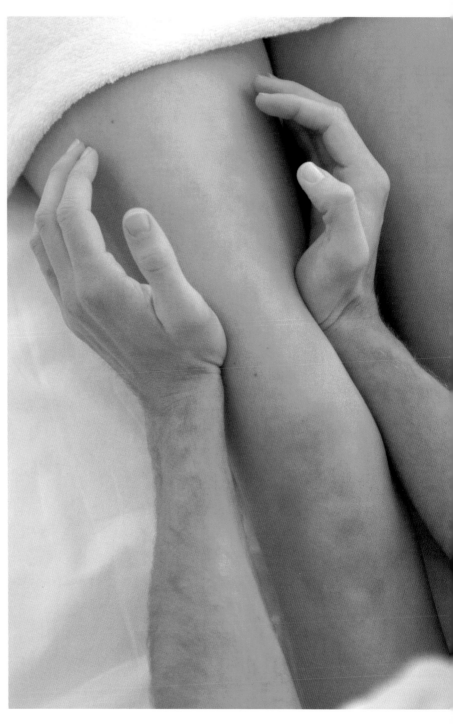

the calves Place both hands on either side of the leg, just below the calf. Tilt your wrists, so that your heels are pressing inward toward each other, and squeeze up and over the calf muscles. Apply pressure in toward the centre. Work in strips up over the calf, always releasing pressure toward the knee.

the thighs Position both hands over the thigh muscles, just above the knee. Using the weight of your body, push upward over the muscles, the heels pressing in toward the centre of the leg. Avoid pressure at the top and inside of the thigh, and round your strokes over the hip. Again, work over the muscles in strips.

rocking

Rocking is a gentle movement that can be applied after you have finished working on one particular area of the body, to complete a massage or in certain cases to loosen up an area beforehand if your partner is particularly tense. Putting both hands on either side of the body, pat alternately toward the centre, so that your partner rocks with your strokes. As well as being fun, it adds a sense of freedom and movement, while relaxing the muscles and loosening the joints. You can rock the limbs one at a time, your hands at different levels up the body, and rock both up and down. Your partner should totally give in to the rocking movement, which is soothing not vigorous. Always end by rocking down the body.

hips and chest Place one hand to the side of your partner's rib cage and place the other on the opposite hip. Gently pat your hands alternately toward the centre of the body, so your partner rocks as you do so. Then slowly move your lower hand upward, bringing the upper hand down to the hip, and return to the starting position.

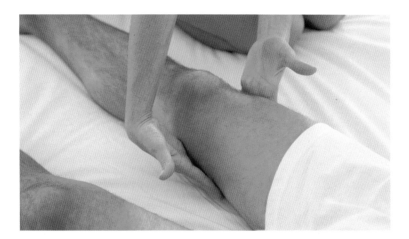

the legs Position both hands at the top of the legs, on either side of the thighs. Gently pat your hands toward each other, travelling simultaneously down the outside of the legs to the feet. The hand movements should be very small at this stage. Return to the top of the legs and then repeat the rocking movement once more.

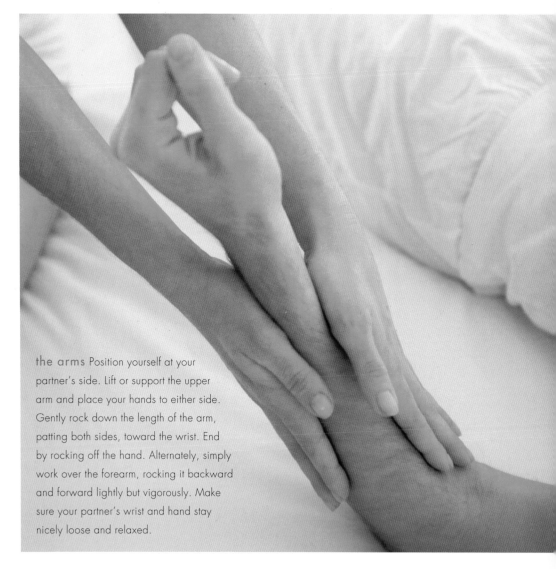

the arms Position yourself at your partner's side. Lift or support the upper arm and place your hands to either side. Gently rock down the length of the arm, patting both sides, toward the wrist. End by rocking off the hand. Alternately, simply work over the forearm, rocking it backward and forward lightly but vigorously. Make sure your partner's wrist and hand stay nicely loose and relaxed.

percussion

Percussion is a term for a particular set of movements, the most common of which are pummelling, hacking and cupping. The movements should be performed quickly and all will have a stimulating effect, increasing the circulation to the surrounding area. Personally, I do not use them very often, but they can be quite fun to stimulate the body after you have worked on a particular area, to change or to quicken the pace of a massage or, in one case I once heard of, to wake the other person up sufficiently that they would not spend hours lingering after the massage! The percussion movements should be performed lightly and sharply and, when done correctly, make a satisfying sound as the hands move over the muscles. Use these strokes over the back, arms, legs and, with caution, over the soles of the feet.

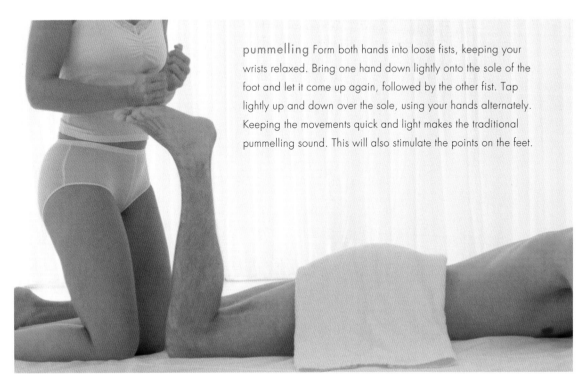

pummelling Form both hands into loose fists, keeping your wrists relaxed. Bring one hand down lightly onto the sole of the foot and let it come up again, followed by the other fist. Tap lightly up and down over the sole, using your hands alternately. Keeping the movements quick and light makes the traditional pummelling sound. This will also stimulate the points on the feet.

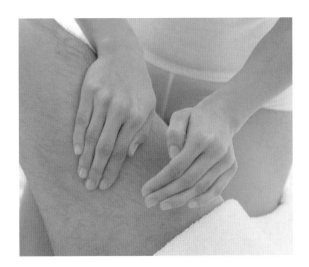

cupping Cup your hands and bring one hand down quickly onto the thigh muscles and up again, followed by the other hand. Move up and down in a series of quick movements. Keep the palm raised, trapping air underneath as you make contact. This produces the cupping sound.

hacking Keeping your hands relaxed, bring the outer side of the hand down quickly onto the shoulder and snap it up again. Repeat the motion with the other hand and then alternate. Chop lightly up and down along the top of the shoulder, keeping the fingers loose to produce the snapping sound.

pressure points

While acupressure is a highly skilled form of massage in itself, a few simple points can be incorporated into a general massage. The principle is based on a series of energy lines, or meridians, running through the body, which relate to all its aspects. Along these lines lie numerous pressure points. If the energy of the meridian is excessive or deficient, pressing the points will help restore the balance, create harmony within the body and prevent disease. I recommend trying the points out first on yourself. They can be located by feeling for a hollow or depression and can be tender. Press in with the thumbs or forefingers, then release the pressure evenly. You may feel a release of energy.

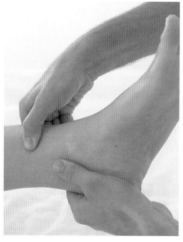

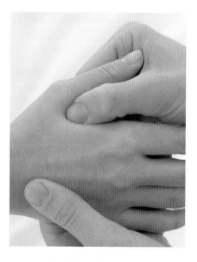

the ball of the foot Locate the ball of the foot and place your thumb just below, in a line downward from the second toe. Press in with the thumb, hold for three seconds and release evenly. This stimulates the Kidney energy and can be used for an immediate energy boost. It has a relaxing and soothing effect.

the inside of the ankle Place your thumb three fingerwidths up from the top of the ankle, just between the bones. Press and hold for three seconds, then release. This point may feel tender. This pressure stimulates the Spleen energy. This point has a calming effect, helps relieve menstrual pains and may stimulate labour.
Note: Do not use during pregnancy.

the web of the thumb Place your thumb in the web between the thumb and first finger, your forefinger underneath. Gently squeeze for three to five seconds, then release. This is known as the 'Great Eliminator' and is on the Large Intestine meridian. It helps eliminate headaches, colds, toothache and constipation.
Note: Do not use during pregnancy.

inner eye corner Place your fingers just above the inner corner of the eyes. Feel for a little notch below the eyebrows in a line up from the eyes. Press carefully with your forefingers, hold for three seconds and release. This point is on the Bladder meridian and helps to relieve headaches. It is quite powerful, so do not press too hard.

centre forehead Place both thumbs in the centre of the forehead, starting just above the eyebrows. Now press gently and release, pressing at regular intervals up toward the hairline. These points lie along the Governing Vessel, which runs down through the centre of the body, and will relieve tension and lift the spirits.

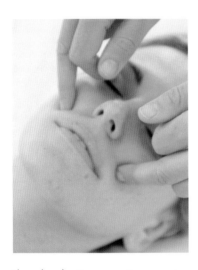

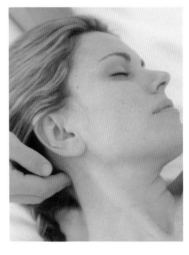

the cheeks Place your fingers under the cheekbones, just to the side of the nose. Trace under the cheeks until you feel a notch about one-third of the way along. Press upward under the bone and release. These points are on the Stomach meridian and help to relieve sinus and general congestion.

the nostrils Place your thumbs to either side of the nose, in the groove just slightly below the edge of the nostrils. Press down, and a fraction in, toward the nose for three seconds, then release. These points lie along the Large Intestine meridian and are good for relieving blocked sinuses and nasal congestion.

the back of the head Rest the head on one hand and with the fingers of the other press in and up under the skull. Begin just to the side of the spine and press at three regular intervals, ending just behind the ear. These points are on the Bladder and Gall Bladder meridians, relieving headaches, tension and colds.

the joints

Any work on the joints involves passive movements, your partner totally relaxing while you manipulate the limbs. It feels good and it stretches and loosens the surrounding soft tissue, which may become tight when the muscles tense up. It is also, I think, a lovely feature of any massage. The key is to make sure your partner gives you their full body weight, while you provide total support, and perform the movements smoothly. Do not go ahead of your partner. If you feel resistance, release the pressure and if your partner tenses up, slow the movement or stop, until the limbs are relaxed once again. Otherwise, your partner will either be doing the movement for you, or it will feel uncomfortable.

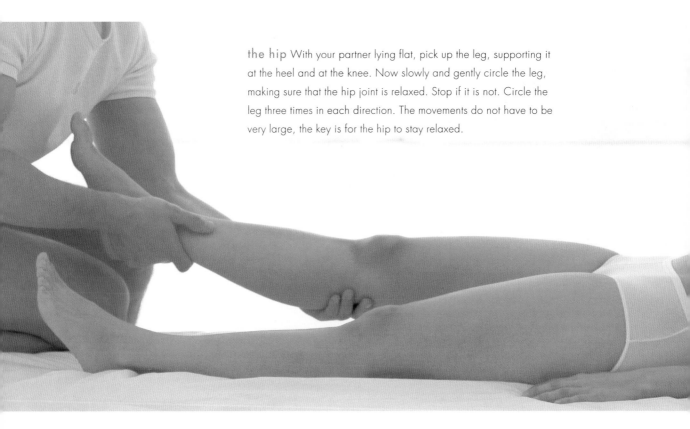

the hip With your partner lying flat, pick up the leg, supporting it at the heel and at the knee. Now slowly and gently circle the leg, making sure that the hip joint is relaxed. Stop if it is not. Circle the leg three times in each direction. The movements do not have to be very large, the key is for the hip to stay relaxed.

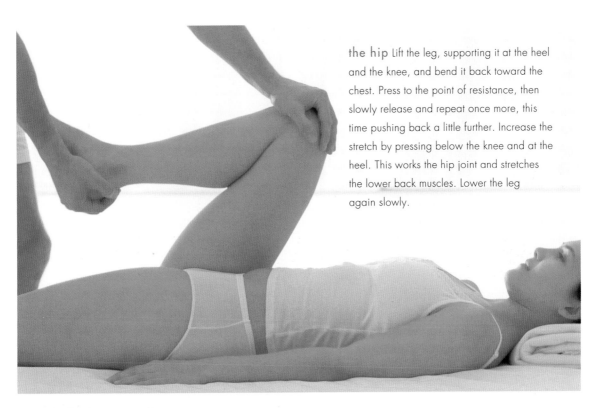

the hip Lift the leg, supporting it at the heel and the knee, and bend it back toward the chest. Press to the point of resistance, then slowly release and repeat once more, this time pushing back a little further. Increase the stretch by pressing below the knee and at the heel. This works the hip joint and stretches the lower back muscles. Lower the leg again slowly.

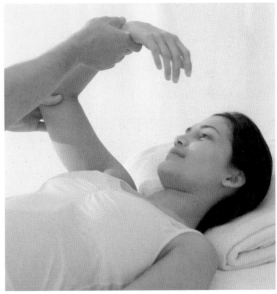

the wrist With the forearm upright and resting on the elbow, take hold of the hand firmly. Now circle the wrist very slowly three times in both directions, bending it each time only as far as feels comfortable. The smoother the rotation, the better. Support the arm with your other hand.

the shoulder With your partner lying flat, lift the arm, supporting it at the wrist and at the elbow. Now circle three times in each direction, guiding the movement with your hands. Make the circles as large as you can, but keep the movement even. Lower the arm afterwards very slowly.

further massage

The following sequence is a more advanced massage, integrating the further techniques with the techniques and steps of the simple massage you are now familiar with. While repeating the strokes already learned does wonders for practice and confidence, this massage provides the opportunity to work in a slightly different way. You will now be working in detail, concentrating on the quality and intensity of your movements, matching the strokes to your partner's muscles. It is important to listen to your partner's body and to know when to continue a stroke and when to stop. As well as massaging the muscles, the new techniques will focus more attention on pressure points and stretches, as well as joints.

the back

In addition to the broad sweeping strokes over the back shown in simple massage, this is now an opportunity to focus in more closely on specific areas, concentrating on the common sites of tension and working much more deeply around the shoulders and lower back. From the very first moment, train your hands to pick up the areas where any tension is held. Feel out your partner's muscle patterns and concentrate on releasing as you stroke. You will begin to get a feel for the strokes that soothe and those that loosen, encouraging tension to disperse. The effleurage and resting strokes have not been included here. Do remember to include these strokes at the beginning and end of every stage.

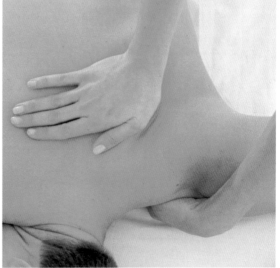

1 **easing the shoulder** First, oil your hands and effleurage the back. Then move to your partner's side and ease gently around the shoulder blade, loosening any tension and generally encouraging the whole area to relax. Use the flat of your hand, concentrating on any spots that feel particularly tight with your fingertips.

2 **pulling the shoulder** This is a slightly different pulling stroke. Place one hand under your partner's shoulder and the other over the top, rather like a sandwich. Pull gently, pulling toward you, rather than up. The shoulder should visibly move as it relaxes. Slide your hands toward you off the shoulder.

3 kneading the shoulder Place your hands over the top of your partner's shoulder. Knead along the muscles to the neck and back out again several times. Push in with your thumbs, particularly where you feel there is any tension, and roll the muscles between your fingers and thumbs as you pull back toward you.

4 pushing across the shoulder Place the tips of your thumbs together just above the shoulder blade. Keeping your thumbs straight, press into the shoulder muscles, starting at the base of the neck and sliding over toward the arm. Ease your pressure at the shoulder joint and repeat the stroke for a very effective tension release.

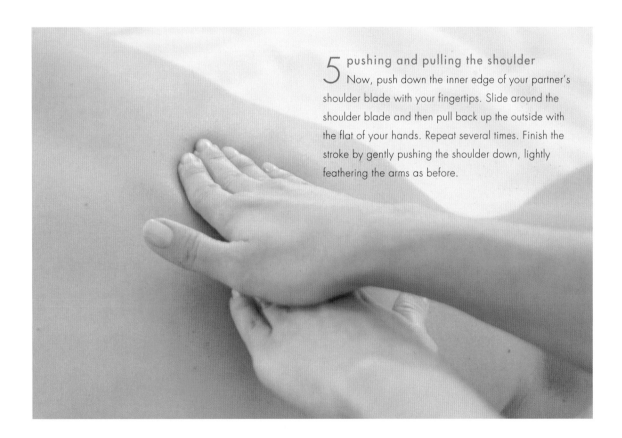

5 pushing and pulling the shoulder Now, push down the inner edge of your partner's shoulder blade with your fingertips. Slide around the shoulder blade and then pull back up the outside with the flat of your hands. Repeat several times. Finish the stroke by gently pushing the shoulder down, lightly feathering the arms as before.

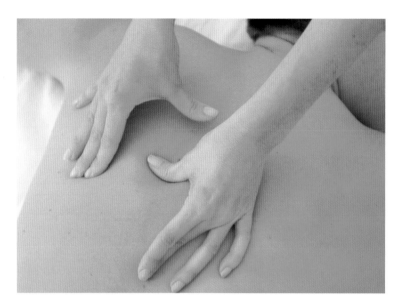

6 rolling down the spine
From the same position, roll your thumbs alternately down the length of your partner's spine to release any tension. Begin just below the base of the neck and roll down the muscles to the side of the spine right to the lower back. As one thumb rolls, the other lifts off. Repeat this several times.

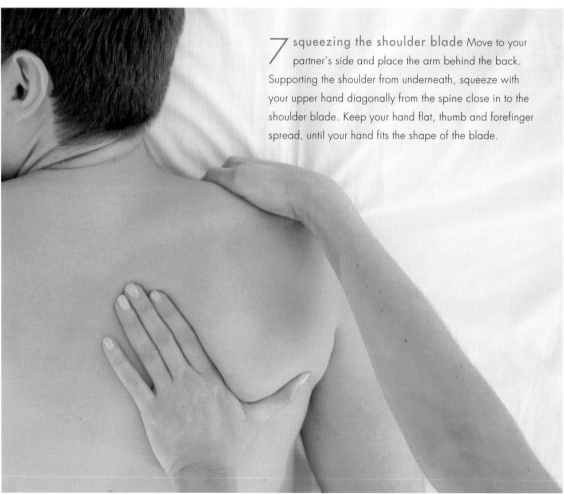

7 squeezing the shoulder blade Move to your partner's side and place the arm behind the back. Supporting the shoulder from underneath, squeeze with your upper hand diagonally from the spine close in to the shoulder blade. Keep your hand flat, thumb and forefinger spread, until your hand fits the shape of the blade.

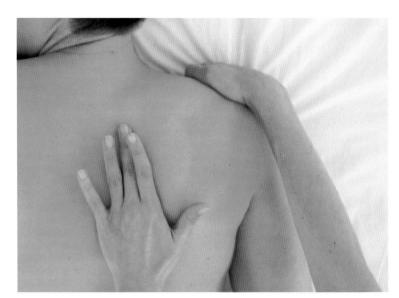

8 pulling around the
  shoulder Place your free hand
over the top of your partner's shoulder,
just at the base of the neck. Curl your
fingers over the muscles, then start
to pull back toward you, drawing
your hand down the inner side of the
shoulder blade. Keep your fingers flat
and apply pressure where you feel
particular tension.

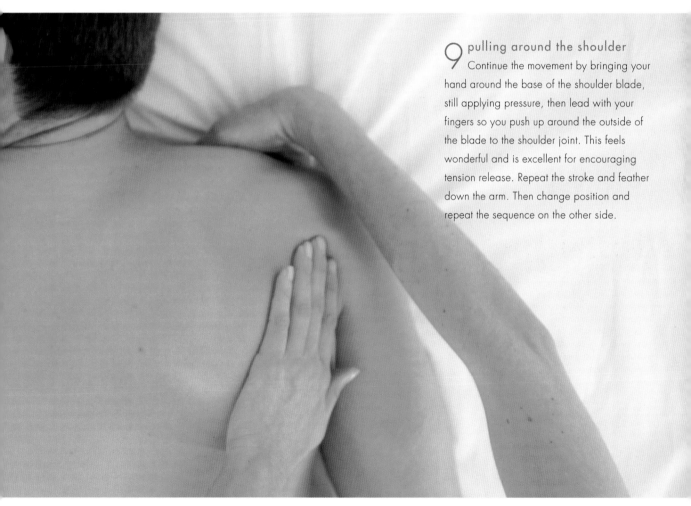

9 pulling around the shoulder
  Continue the movement by bringing your
hand around the base of the shoulder blade,
still applying pressure, then lead with your
fingers so you push up around the outside of
the blade to the shoulder joint. This feels
wonderful and is excellent for encouraging
tension release. Repeat the stroke and feather
down the arm. Then change position and
repeat the sequence on the other side.

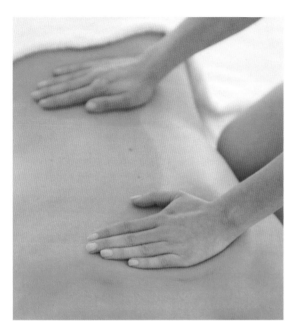

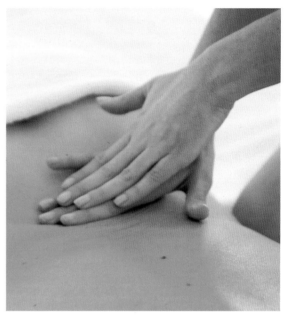

10 lower back stretch First effleurage the lower back. Place both hands together in the middle of the back and slide one hand down toward the sacrum (the bony triangle at the base of the spine). Continue the stretch over the sacrum, pulling your other hand gently in the opposite direction. Do this once, carefully.

11 circling the sacrum Place both hands, one on top of the other, over your partner's sacrum. Slowly circle anticlockwise, keeping both hands flat and using your upper hand for pressure. Make the circles quite large to release the tension in the lower back. Always check the pressure in this area with your partner.

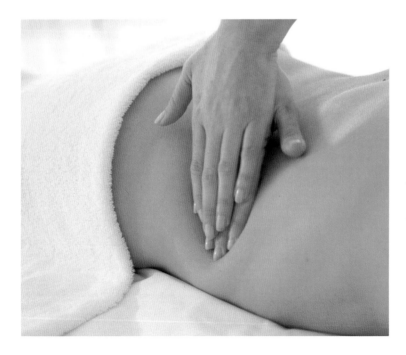

12 pulling around the hip Place both hands to the far side of your partner's spine, just above the hip. Push both hands downward over the back, stretching the muscles away from you. Continue by circling around the hip and drawing back up over the buttock. Use the flat of your hands for the first stage of the movement, finishing with pressure from the heels. Repeat several times.

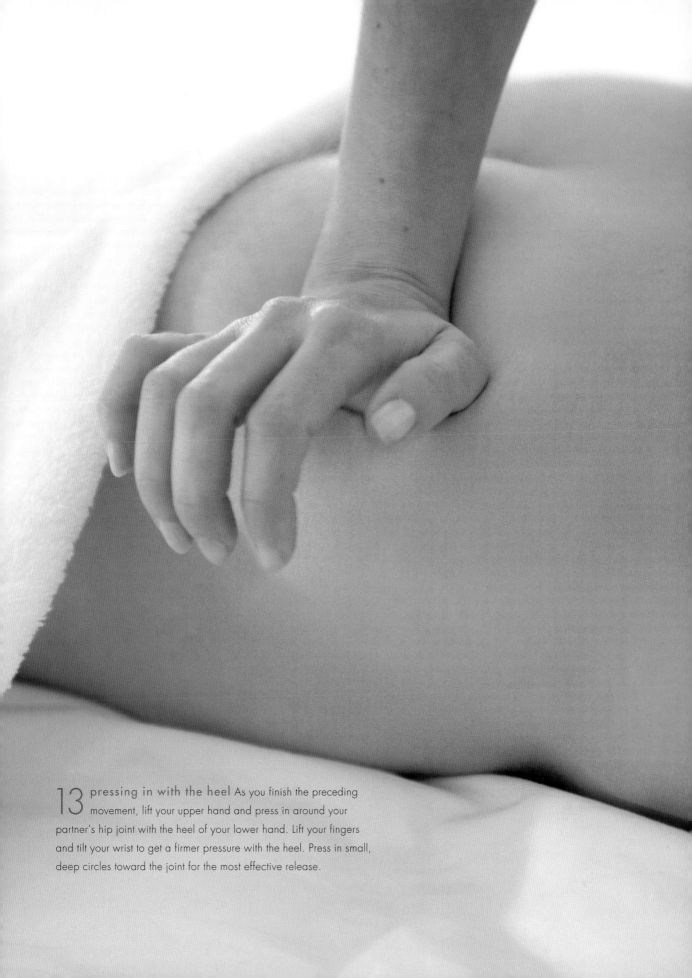

13 pressing in with the heel As you finish the preceding
movement, lift your upper hand and press in around your
partner's hip joint with the heel of your lower hand. Lift your fingers
and tilt your wrist to get a firmer pressure with the heel. Press in small,
deep circles toward the joint for the most effective release.

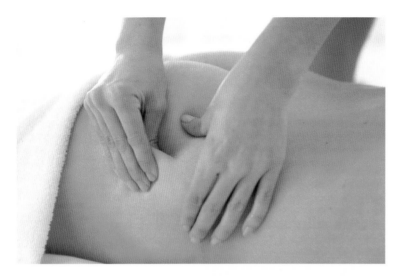

14 **kneading** Begin kneading over your partner's buttock to really loosen the muscles. Press in with your thumb and roll back toward you with the fingers. Use quite firm pressure over the soft area of muscle, working in an alternating rhythm with your hands. Focus particularly on any tight spots.

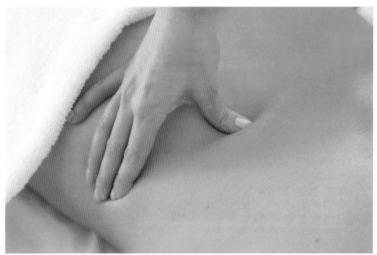

15 **thumb circling** Place your thumb at the top of your partner's sacrum and just to the far side of the spine. Using the tip of your thumb make small circular movements outward over the sacrum. Check the pressure with your partner. Then repeat, each time beginning slightly further down the spine.

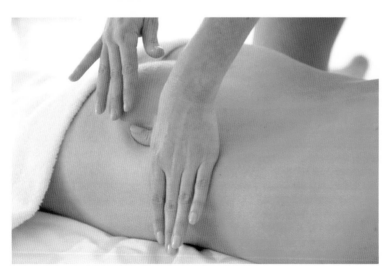

16 **thumb rolling** Roll both thumbs diagonally over the buttock, moving from the sacrum toward the hip. Alternate your thumbs as you roll, so the movement feels like a continuous wave. Ensure you only press over the soft muscle, repeating the rolls several times. This feels good and helps the tension to disperse.

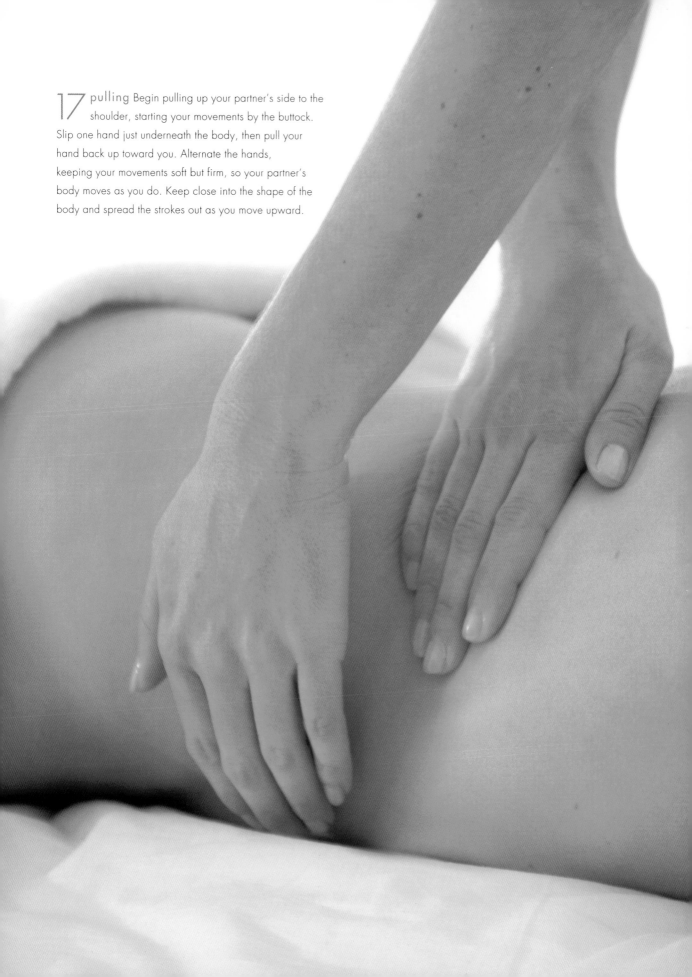

17 **pulling** Begin pulling up your partner's side to the shoulder, starting your movements by the buttock. Slip one hand just underneath the body, then pull your hand back up toward you. Alternate the hands, keeping your movements soft but firm, so your partner's body moves as you do. Keep close into the shape of the body and spread the strokes out as you move upward.

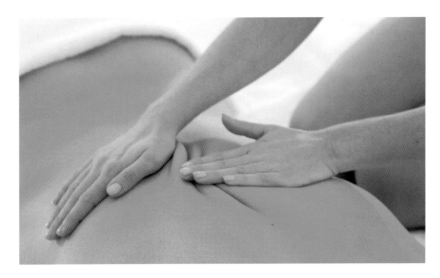

18 wringing Place one hand to the far side of your partner's lower back, the other just above the hip nearest you. Start to pull your far hand back toward you, the other hand pushing away. The muscles will twist as your hands cross over and slide to opposite sides. Repeat several times up and down the lower back.

19 forearm stretch Lean over your partner. Rest both forearms together in the middle of the back, facing each other, to the far side of the spine. Turn your forearms over and then slowly draw them apart until you reach the shoulder and hip. Lean into the stroke to provide a good stretch. Then repeat each step on the other side.

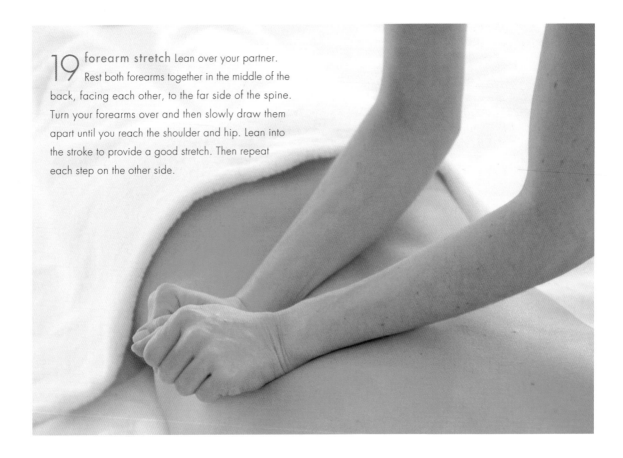

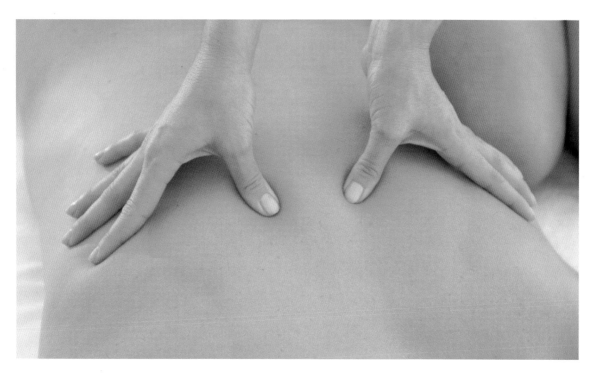

20 circling up the spine Place both hands together at the base of your partner's spine, the pads of your thumbs over the muscles to either side. Now start making circular movements up over the muscles, your hands gliding toward the neck. Push then circle in continuous strokes and release gently at the base of the skull.

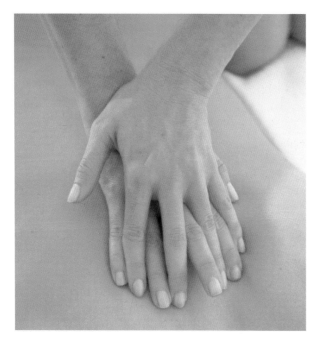

21 raking the spine Put both hands together at the top of the spine and rake down to the lower back. Use the pads of your fingers to draw down the muscles alongside the spine. This releases tension and heightens your partner's body awareness. Repeat several times, stroke down the spine, then rest your hands over the back.

the back of the legs

Now that you possess an increased sensitivity and knowledge of your partner's muscles, you can work on the areas of the legs where you feel the tension in greater depth. The use of the thumbs and heels of the hands allows your strokes to penetrate more deeply. Some strokes to loosen the joints are now included, which is a particular feature of this massage. You will still need to take care and check the pressure with your partner frequently. Some women may find their calves quite painful, and the outer thighs can also be tender. If your partner's thighs are ticklish, keep your strokes firm and concise. Always check whether your partner has any hip or knee problems before performing any stretches.

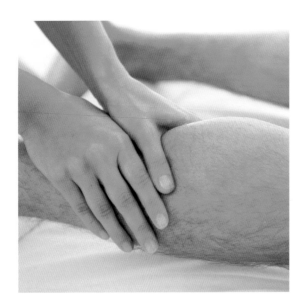

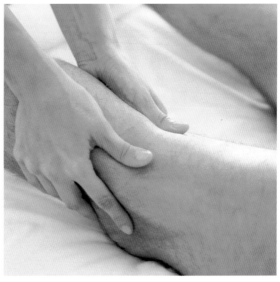

1 **squeezing the calf** Effleurage the leg. Then, place your hand over the calf, thumb on one side and fingers on the other. Begin squeezing up the calf muscles, this time working on any tight areas with your thumb. Rub, press and squeeze the muscles to loosen them, using both hands for pressure. Ease toward the knee.

2 **drawing over knee** Cup your hands around your partner's leg, with your thumbs together in the centre of the crease at the back of the knee. Slowly move your hands apart, drawing lightly over the crease with your thumbs. This stroke not only feels delightful, but will release any tension right around the joint.

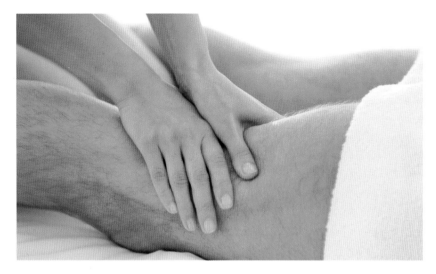

3 **squeezing the thigh** Bring your hands together over the back of
the thigh, starting just above the knee. Spread your hands wide so your
thumbs are on one side of the muscles, your fingers on the other. Really lean
into the stroke and use your body weight to squeeze up over the thigh,
releasing your pressure toward the buttock. Repeat several times.

4 **heel squeeze** Use the heel of your hand to squeeze up the outside
of your partner's thigh. Tilt your wrist back and lift your fingers in order to
apply a firm pressure with the heel of the hand. Begin just above the knee and
squeeze the thigh in a continuous stroke up the outside of the leg, rounding
off over the hip. Then repeat.

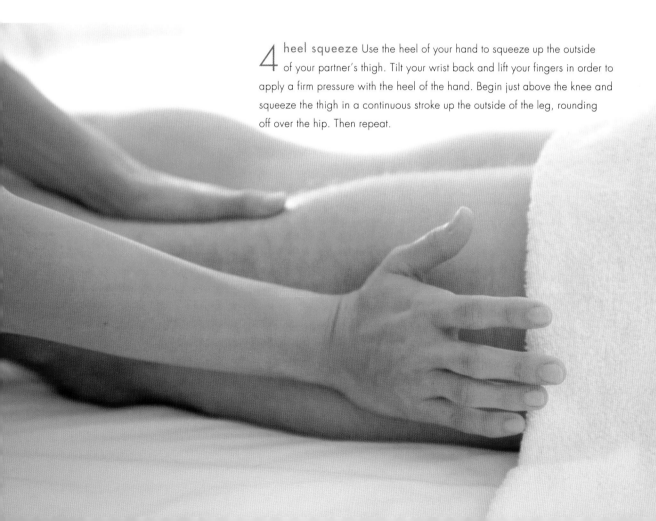

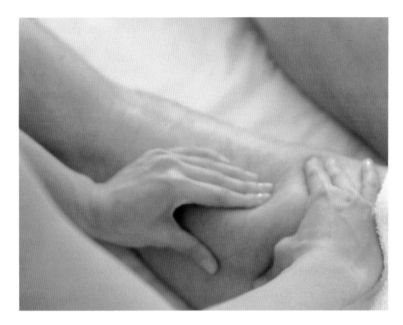

5 kneading the thigh Begin kneading over the back and outer thigh, pressing in with your thumbs and rolling the muscles back toward you. Move up and down over the leg, feeling for tight spots with your hands and concentrating on any areas where you feel there is tension. Ease your pressure toward the knee and hip.

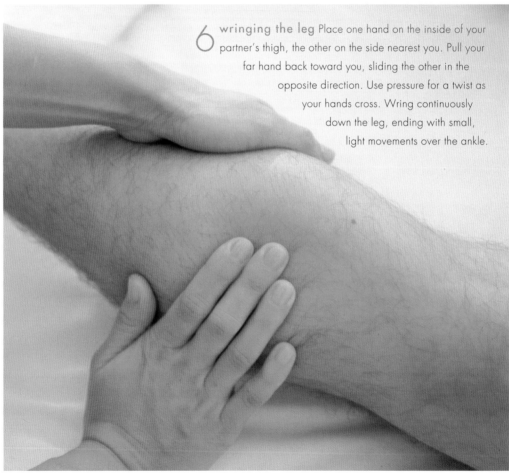

6 wringing the leg Place one hand on the inside of your partner's thigh, the other on the side nearest you. Pull your far hand back toward you, sliding the other in the opposite direction. Use pressure for a twist as your hands cross. Wring continuously down the leg, ending with small, light movements over the ankle.

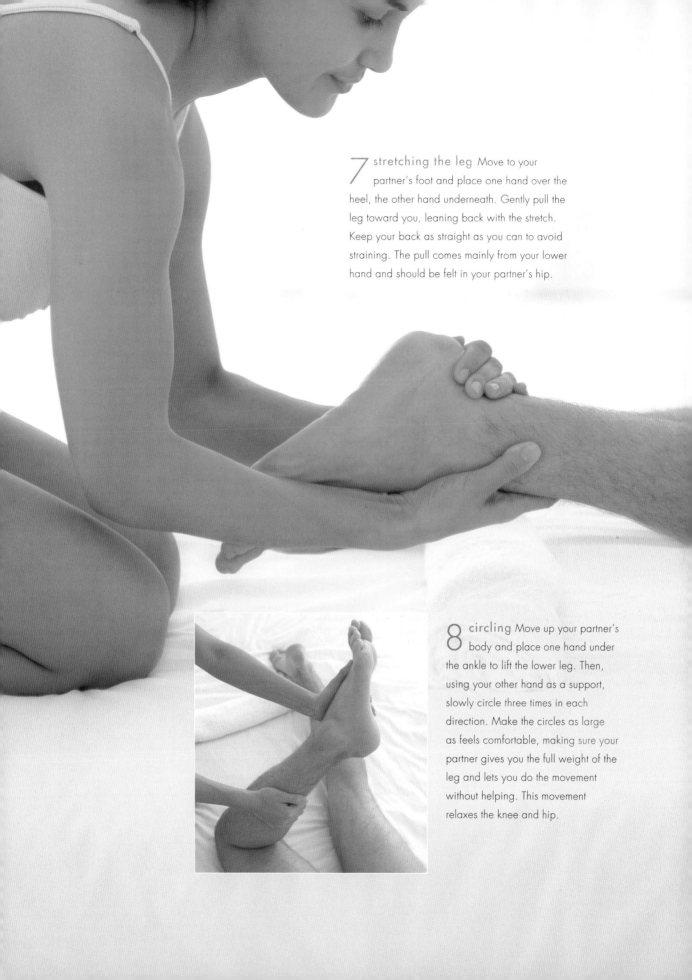

7 **stretching the leg** Move to your partner's foot and place one hand over the heel, the other hand underneath. Gently pull the leg toward you, leaning back with the stretch. Keep your back as straight as you can to avoid straining. The pull comes mainly from your lower hand and should be felt in your partner's hip.

8 **circling** Move up your partner's body and place one hand under the ankle to lift the lower leg. Then, using your other hand as a support, slowly circle three times in each direction. Make the circles as large as feels comfortable, making sure your partner gives you the full weight of the leg and lets you do the movement without helping. This movement relaxes the knee and hip.

the feet

The feet and ankles complete the massage on the back of the body in a very real sense. Proper attention to the feet is an essential part of receiving a full body massage, of being worked on from head to toe. This position is effective for massaging the sole of the foot, as well as for the passive movements on the ankle joint. The soles of the feet are very sensitive, with many nerve endings as well as reflex zones, so massage here can affect the organs of the body as well as being very relaxing. Make sure you work over the feet thoroughly to give a sense of completeness, but be careful around the instep, where pressure should be minimal. Ticklishness can often be helped by conscious relaxation.

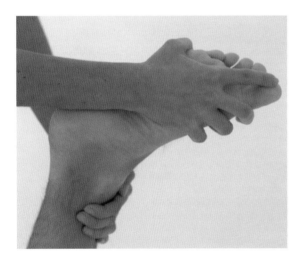

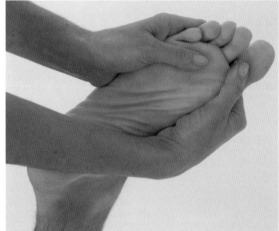

1 **rotating the ankle** With your partner's leg still raised and supported by your hand, place the other hand over the sole of the foot. With your fingers grasping the ball of the foot, rest your forearm over the heel and begin to rotate the ankle slowly. Using your forearm as a lever in order to help the movement, circle the foot as far and completely as possible. Repeat the movement three times in each direction.

2 **twisting the foot** Hold the sides of your partner's foot between the palms of your hands. Apply pressure by pulling down with the fingers of one hand and pushing upward with the heel of the other in order to turn the foot. Press to the point of resistance and then repeat the action the other way. This helps to stretch the muscles and will give your partner a good feeling of release.

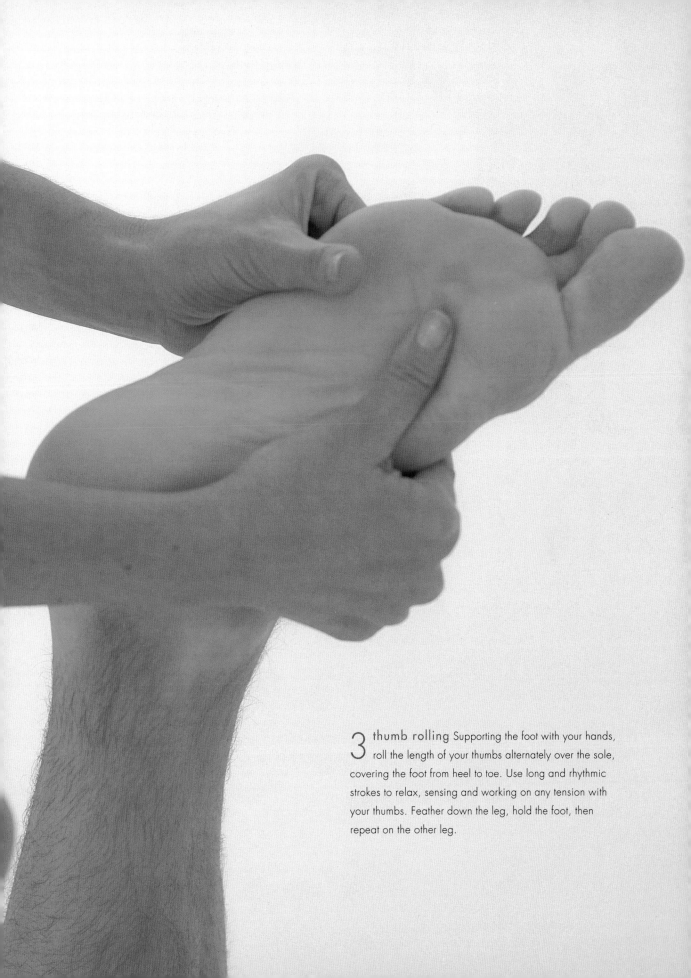

3 thumb rolling Supporting the foot with your hands, roll the length of your thumbs alternately over the sole, covering the foot from heel to toe. Use long and rhythmic strokes to relax, sensing and working on any tension with your thumbs. Feather down the leg, hold the foot, then repeat on the other leg.

the neck

This part of the massage gives you the chance to really work both on the neck muscles and at stretching out the spine. In fact, I would never give a back massage without working on the neck. As you massage, have the sense of loosening the muscles and of releasing the tension up the neck, as well as concentrating on movement and flexibility. Tension in the back and shoulders nearly always affects the neck, which in turn can be the cause of headaches. The final releasing movements over the head can often soothe away such aches and pains. Take plenty of time when massaging your partner's neck. Of all the areas of the body, back and neck massages are the most beneficial and appreciated.

1 **neck stretch** Sit at your partner's head and rub a little oil onto your hands. Place your fingertips at the top of the chest and draw the tips outward over the shoulders and up the back of the neck, cupping your hands around the base of the skull. Pull directly back toward you, tilting the chin downward and lengthening the spine as you do so. Allow your fingers to slide underneath the skull and then release.

2 **rolling the neck** Place both hands to either side of your partner's neck. Now roll one hand upward along the neck muscles, turning your partner's head the opposite way as you do so. Support the neck with your free hand. Repeat the movement with the other hand, turning your partner's head back again. Gently roll the head from side to side several times, making sure your partner stays totally relaxed.

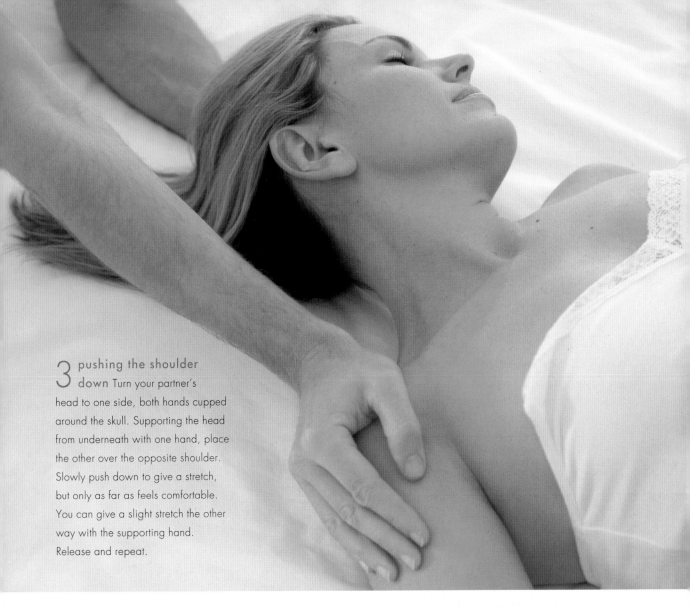

3 **pushing the shoulder down** Turn your partner's head to one side, both hands cupped around the skull. Supporting the head from underneath with one hand, place the other over the opposite shoulder. Slowly push down to give a stretch, but only as far as feels comfortable. You can give a slight stretch the other way with the supporting hand. Release and repeat.

4 **pulling up the side of the neck** Keeping your supporting hand beneath your partner's head, slide your free hand under the back as far as you can. (Your partner should not move to help you.) Make sure you are to the side of the spine. Press in with your fingers and pull back up the muscles right to the base of the skull. Your pressure should be more gentle on the neck. Repeat for a deep tension release.

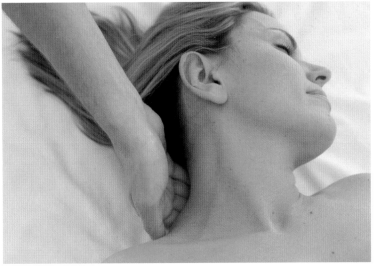

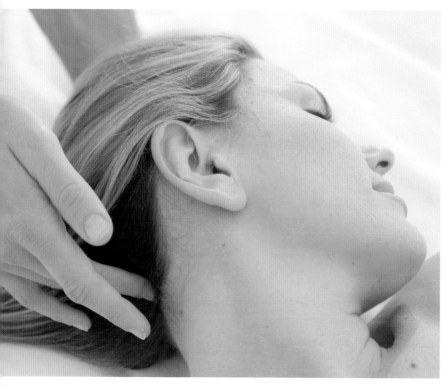

5 **pressing under the skull**
Locate the bony ridge at the base of your partner's skull. Then, place your fingertips underneath, just to the side of the spine. Gently press your fingertips inward, pressing up under the skull. Increase the pressure if your partner feels comfortable, then release. Continue to press and release evenly at regular intervals, following the ridge to the ear.

6 **rotating the scalp** Arch your hand, placing the tips of your fingers over your partner's scalp. Pressing down with the fingertips, rotate your hand on the spot over the scalp. This should be a careful and precise movement. The skin should move as you do so. Lift your hand and repeat the movement. Work firmly over the scalp, without altering the position of your fingers.

7 pulling the hair Shampoo firmly
over your partner's head. To end,
very gently run your fingers through the
hair and tug lightly at the roots. Repeat
the movement over the scalp, grasping
the hair firmly and giving a slight pull. This
not only feels wonderful, but relaxes and
stimulates the scalp. End by pulling a few
strands gently, then repeat the movements
on the other side.

the face

When you massage the face, you will be working over a few of its many pressure points. As the movements over the face are quite precise, your fingers need to be sensitive both to the position of the muscles and to picking up their response. Feel out each area you work on with your fingertips, using the bone structure to help you. When you are massaging your partner's forehead, keep your mind as clear as possible, in order to help your partner relax. A calm mind and a steady touch will affect your partner more than you might think. Again, make sure your movements end with an upward motion. If your partner's eyes start rolling under the eyelids, you can take this as a very good sign!

1 **drawing across the forehead** Rest both hands at the side of your partner's head and place your thumbs together in the centre of the forehead. Slowly draw the thumbs apart, smoothing across the forehead to the hairline. Apply gentle pressure with the length of the thumbs, releasing lightly at the end of the stroke. Repeat twice.

2 **pressing the eye sockets** With the tips of your forefingers, gently press upward just under the eye socket ridge. Begin at the nose, below the inner part of the eyebrows, and work outward along the eye, pressing at small, regular intervals. Follow the natural curve to the outer corner, avoiding any direct contact with the eye itself.

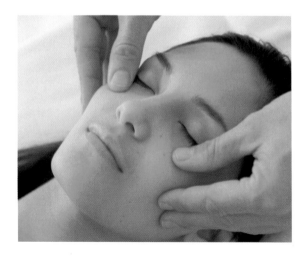

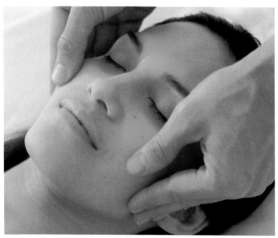

3 pressing the eye sockets Continue the movement just beneath the lower eye socket ridge. Start at the outer corner and press at regular intervals along the line of the bone, this time using the pads of your thumbs. Work back toward the nose, avoiding contact with the eye, and release pressure at the inner corner.

4 drawing under the cheeks Rest your hands at the side of your partner's face. Place the pads of your thumbs just under the cheekbones and draw outward from the nose toward the jaw. Gently press in and slightly upward under the bone, drawing the movement outward without stretching the skin. Release pressure toward the ears.

5 drawing out across the cheeks Place your hands just above the cheekbones and using the sides of the balls of the thumbs, draw out across the cheeks toward the ears. Use a very precise pressure. Return to the nose, place your thumbs slightly higher up the cheeks, then repeat the stroke. Work in small strips upward over the cheeks.

6 **jaw pinching** Place your hands in the centre of your partner's chin, thumbs just above the chin and fingers underneath. Gently pinch the muscles and soft tissue between thumbs and forefingers and continue to squeeze at regular intervals, working outward along the jaw line. Continue squeezing until you reach the angle of the jaw.

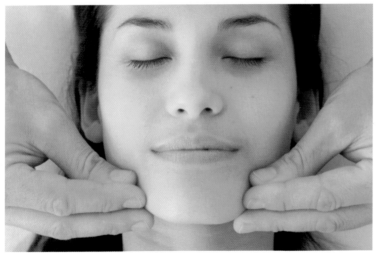

7 **drawing under the chin** Return to the centre of your partner's chin. Cup your hands around the chin, fingertips now touching in the middle. Slowly draw your hands apart, moving out toward the ears. Draw both above and below the jaw line. This is a long, slow stroke, excellent for helping to disperse any tension.

8 **circling the jaw** Now, slide your fingertips into position over your partner's jaw muscles. Slowly begin to circle the fingertips toward you over the jaw muscles so that the strokes really penetrate. If the muscles feel tight, encourage your partner to relax. Opening the jaw slightly will assist in relaxation. This stroke can relieve stress and is also useful in helping to reduce headaches.

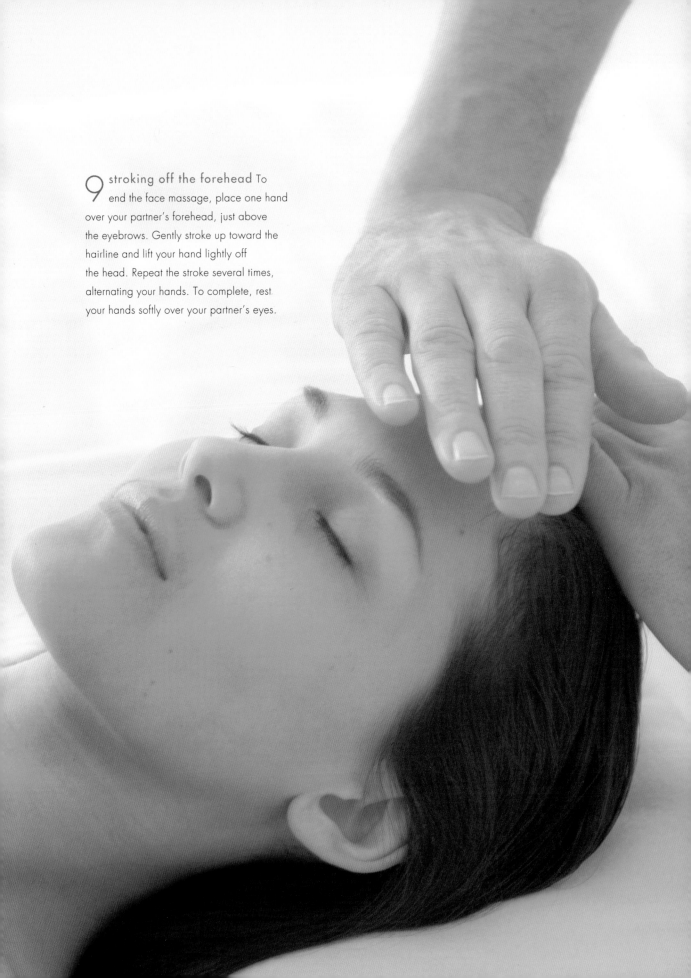

9 **stroking off the forehead** To end the face massage, place one hand over your partner's forehead, just above the eyebrows. Gently stroke up toward the hairline and lift your hand lightly off the head. Repeat the stroke several times, alternating your hands. To complete, rest your hands softly over your partner's eyes.

the arms

Now the squeezing movements will cover a greater proportion of the arms. You can use this opportunity to become more sensitive to the muscles, feeling for any tension with your fingertips, and using the strokes with greater precision and effectiveness. The circling and stretching movements will promote general flexibility and a sense of freedom, particularly helping to loosen the shoulders. Always keep your movements smooth and confident in order to encourage your partner to relax. If you feel your partner tensing or holding on, slow right down or stop, until you feel the muscles let go. This way, your partner is truly learning to relax, which will greatly affect the benefits of the massage.

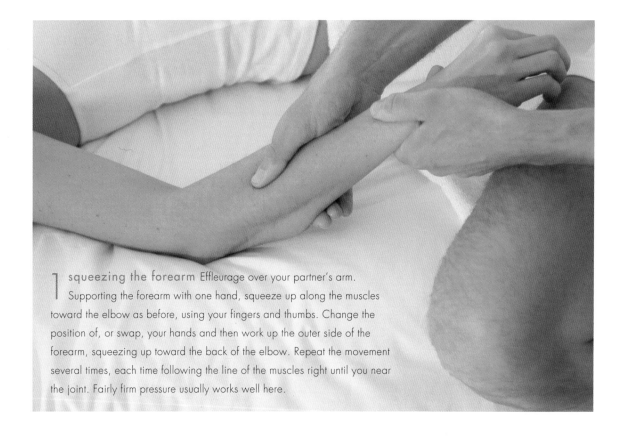

1 **squeezing the forearm** Effleurage over your partner's arm. Supporting the forearm with one hand, squeeze up along the muscles toward the elbow as before, using your fingers and thumbs. Change the position of, or swap, your hands and then work up the outer side of the forearm, squeezing up toward the back of the elbow. Repeat the movement several times, each time following the line of the muscles right until you near the joint. Fairly firm pressure usually works well here.

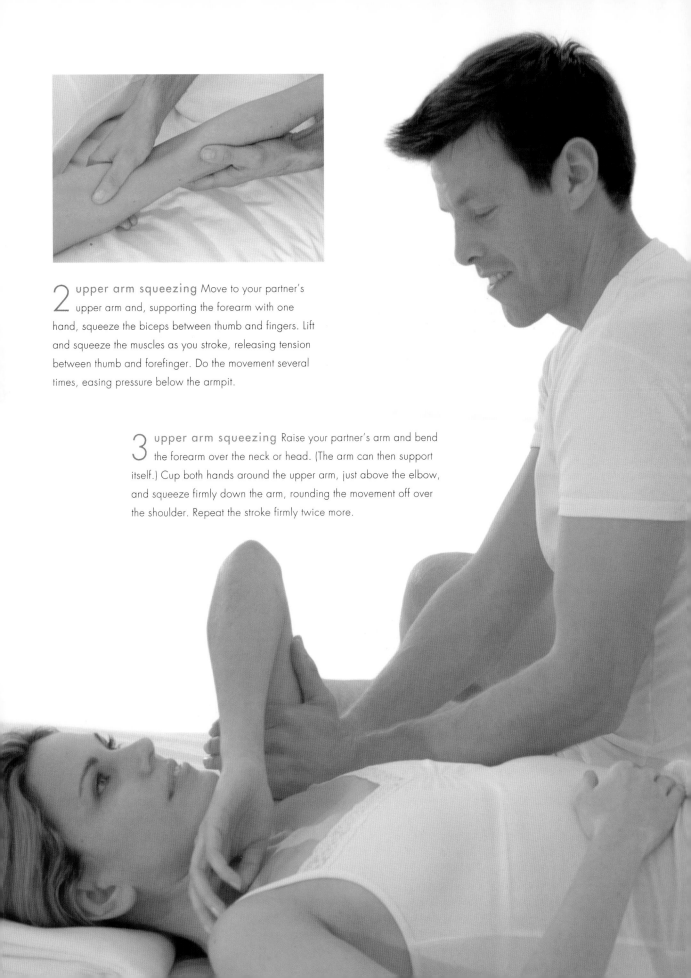

2 **upper arm squeezing** Move to your partner's upper arm and, supporting the forearm with one hand, squeeze the biceps between thumb and fingers. Lift and squeeze the muscles as you stroke, releasing tension between thumb and forefinger. Do the movement several times, easing pressure below the armpit.

3 **upper arm squeezing** Raise your partner's arm and bend the forearm over the neck or head. (The arm can then support itself.) Cup both hands around the upper arm, just above the elbow, and squeeze firmly down the arm, rounding the movement off over the shoulder. Repeat the stroke firmly twice more.

4 **arm circling** Lift your partner's arm, one hand at the wrist and the other supporting at the elbow. Slowly circle the arm outward, making sure the movement comes from a relaxed shoulder joint. Guide the arm with your hands, making wide, comfortable circles. Circle three times.

5 **stretching** Now stretch your partner's arm up as before, grasping at the wrist and supporting at the elbow. At the top of the stretch, pull the arm backward, so you stretch behind your partner's head. Let the arm relax, then pull up and backward once more.

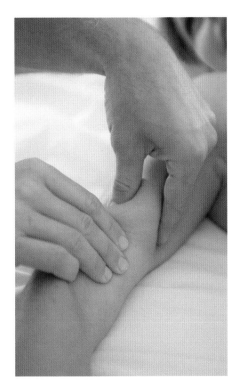

6 **upper arm kneading** Lay your partner's arm flat and begin kneading over the muscles at the front of the arm. Push with your thumbs and roll the muscles back toward you, concentrating on tight spots. Knead over the muscles several times, keeping your movements small.

7 **opening the hand** Cup your hands around the upper arm, thumbs together in the centre, facing toward you. Slowly draw your thumbs apart, pressing with the base. Repeat the stroke down the arm. Now draw out in the same way over the top of the hand, arching it with your fingers and the base of your thumbs.

the hands

Most people will willingly have their hands massaged. There are many
pressure points and reflex zones on the hands in the same way as there
are in the feet. They are very sensitive and respond well to touch. Take
time to work thoroughly over the palms, massaging the wrist and finger
joints. Do the movements slowly and with care to get the maximum release.
You will need to find a balance between being delicate and effective with
your strokes. By massaging the hands you can release tension through
the fingertips and the final stroke will lift and stimulate. Massaging the
extremities is an important part of a body massage. Bringing the attention
to each part of the body creates a sense of thoroughness.

1 **circling the palm** Turn your partner's hand over
and hold it in your own. Then, pressing into the palm
with the pad of your thumb, make small circular movements
on the spot, pressing in an outward direction. Press as you
circle for increased penetration. Cover the surface of the
palm, including the base of the thumb, using both hands
if it feels easier.

2 **rotating the wrist** Support the forearm with one
hand and with the other grasp your partner's hand.
Then, bring the hand forward as far as comfortable and
slowly start to circle it. Make the circles as full as possible.
Rotate the wrist twice in each direction, applying more
pressure to the hand where necessary.

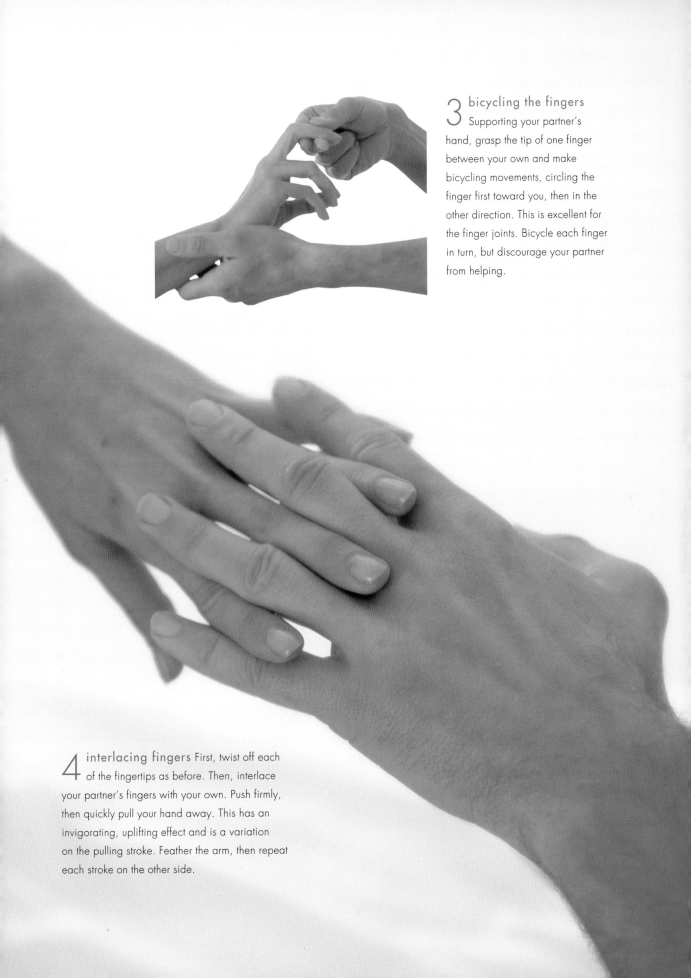

3 bicycling the fingers
Supporting your partner's hand, grasp the tip of one finger between your own and make bicycling movements, circling the finger first toward you, then in the other direction. This is excellent for the finger joints. Bicycle each finger in turn, but discourage your partner from helping.

4 interlacing fingers First, twist off each of the fingertips as before. Then, interlace your partner's fingers with your own. Push firmly, then quickly pull your hand away. This has an invigorating, uplifting effect and is a variation on the pulling stroke. Feather the arm, then repeat each stroke on the other side.

the chest

A variety of new massage strokes are used over the chest, in particular working on the pectoral muscles, over the rib cage and between the ribs. The chest muscles on a man can be quite developed, so you may need to work at encouraging general relaxation. If the breath is being held in any way, encourage your partner to let go and breathe naturally. The key here is to release the muscles in the upper chest, give liberating stretches along the rib cage and work closely between the ribs. This combination will give the feeling of openness and expansion, and it allows the rib cage to move more freely. It may take time to familiarize yourself with the new massage strokes and to achieve the best effect.

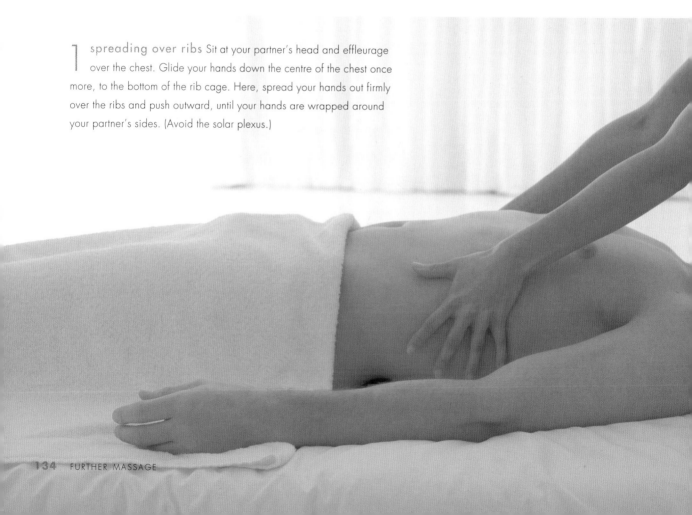

1 spreading over ribs Sit at your partner's head and effleurage over the chest. Glide your hands down the centre of the chest once more, to the bottom of the rib cage. Here, spread your hands out firmly over the ribs and push outward, until your hands are wrapped around your partner's sides. (Avoid the solar plexus.)

2 circling From this position, start to circle up the sides of your partner's body, toward you. Keep your hands flat against the sides of the ribs and make big, slow circles, travelling up the body toward the armpits. Return to the lower ribs and repeat the stroke once again. You will need to check that you keep your balance as you do this. Circle three times up your partner's body giving a little stretch along the ribs each time you do so.

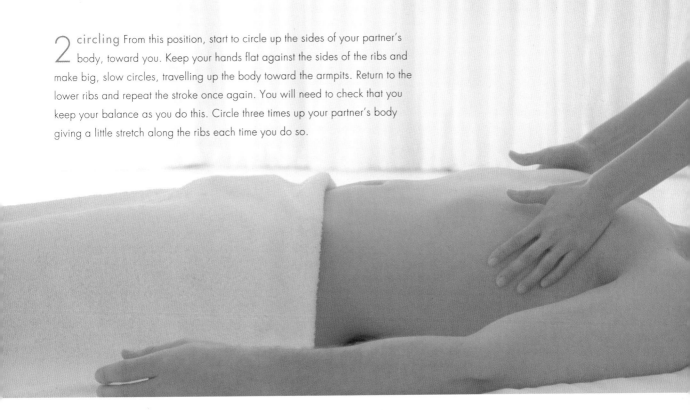

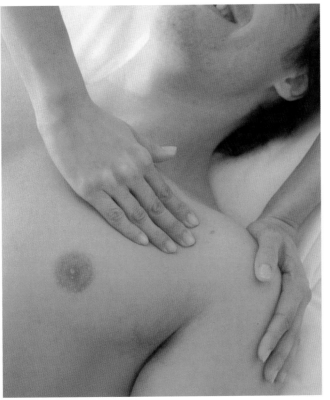

3 chest push Use one hand as a supporting hand and then place the fingertips of the other at the top of your partner's chest, just to the side of the breastbone. Push firmly with your fingers out along the ribs toward the shoulder joint. Repeat twice more, each time slightly further down the chest. If your partner is a woman, take care not to massage directly over the breasts. It always feels good when you press between the ribs.

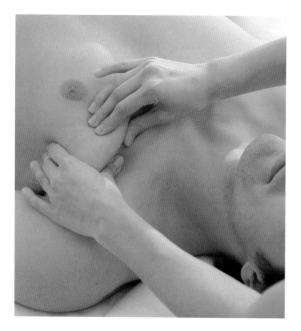

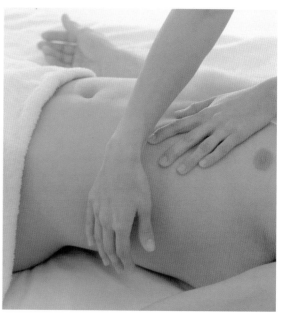

4 **kneading the pectorals** Lean across your partner and carefully begin to knead the pectoral muscles, avoiding massaging over the nipples. Push in and then roll the muscles back toward you with your fingers. If your partner is a woman, the actual area you can massage will naturally be smaller. Firm strokes over the pectoral muscles will be particularly releasing.

5 **pulling up the ribs** Lean further across your partner, placing one hand just under the rib cage. Pull your hand back up toward you, then repeat the movement with your other hand. Pull up alternately toward the centre of the chest, and then round off the movement at the shoulder. Repeat these last three strokes on the other side.

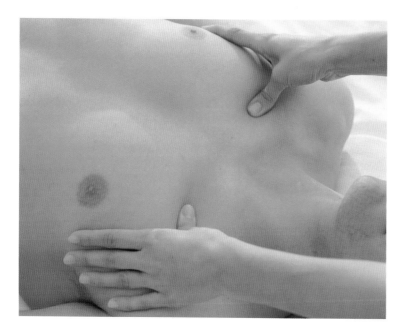

6 **drawing out across the ribs** Place the pads of your thumbs either side of your partner's breastbone, in the groove just beneath the collarbone. Now, push firmly out toward the shoulder joint with both thumbs at the same time, gradually releasing the pressure toward the end of the stroke. Repeat slowly twice more, the last time rounding your stroke off over the shoulder. This movement will give your partner a wonderful feeling of release across the chest.

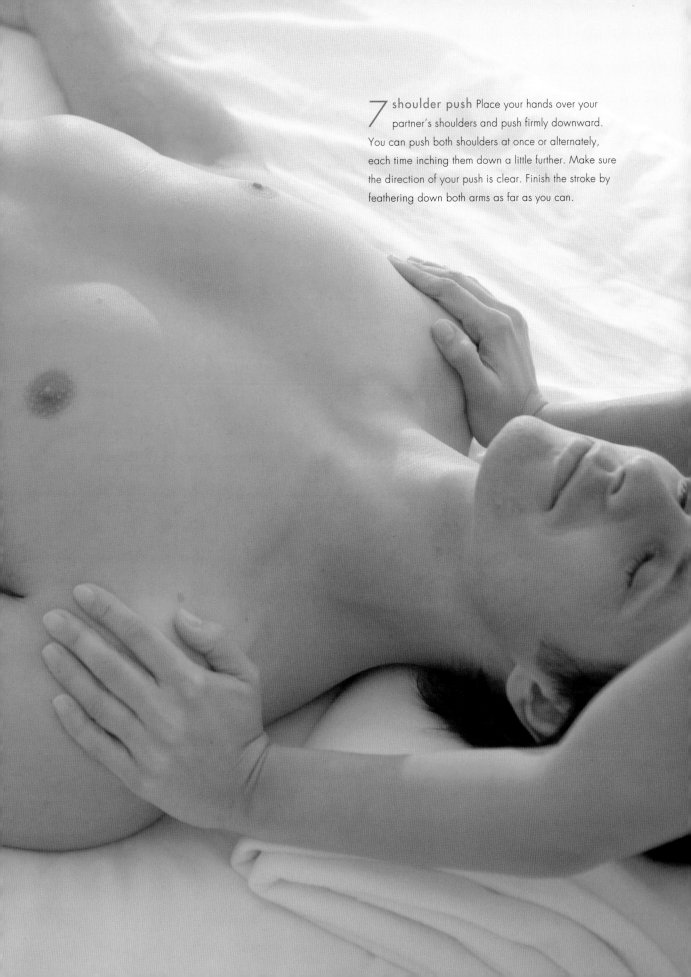

7 **shoulder push** Place your hands over your partner's shoulders and push firmly downward. You can push both shoulders at once or alternately, each time inching them down a little further. Make sure the direction of your push is clear. Finish the stroke by feathering down both arms as far as you can.

the abdomen

You can now add deeper and more specific pressure circling, as well as kneading, to your basic strokes over the abdomen. However, as this is a sensitive, unprotected area of the body, you should never massage really deeply. For men especially, this can be particularly sensitive sexually, so use your discretion and shorten the massage if necessary. Your strokes should never be intrusive. Within the abdomen are vital pressure points and energy centres related to organ movement, which may have become restricted due to stress. A soothing, confident massage can have really sensational results, both releasing energy and bringing the breath down to the abdomen, restoring natural breathing patterns.

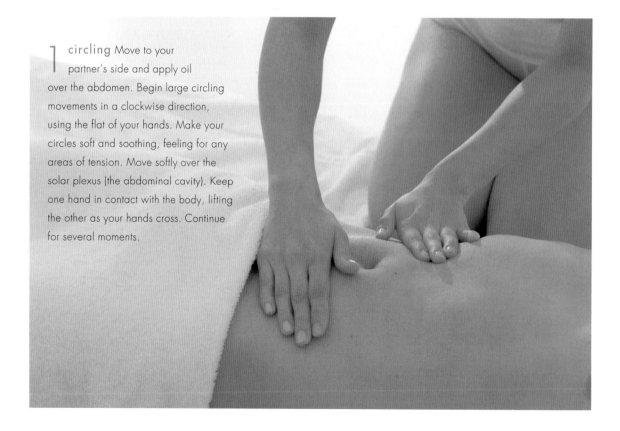

1 circling Move to your partner's side and apply oil over the abdomen. Begin large circling movements in a clockwise direction, using the flat of your hands. Make your circles soft and soothing, feeling for any areas of tension. Move softly over the solar plexus (the abdominal cavity). Keep one hand in contact with the body, lifting the other as your hands cross. Continue for several moments.

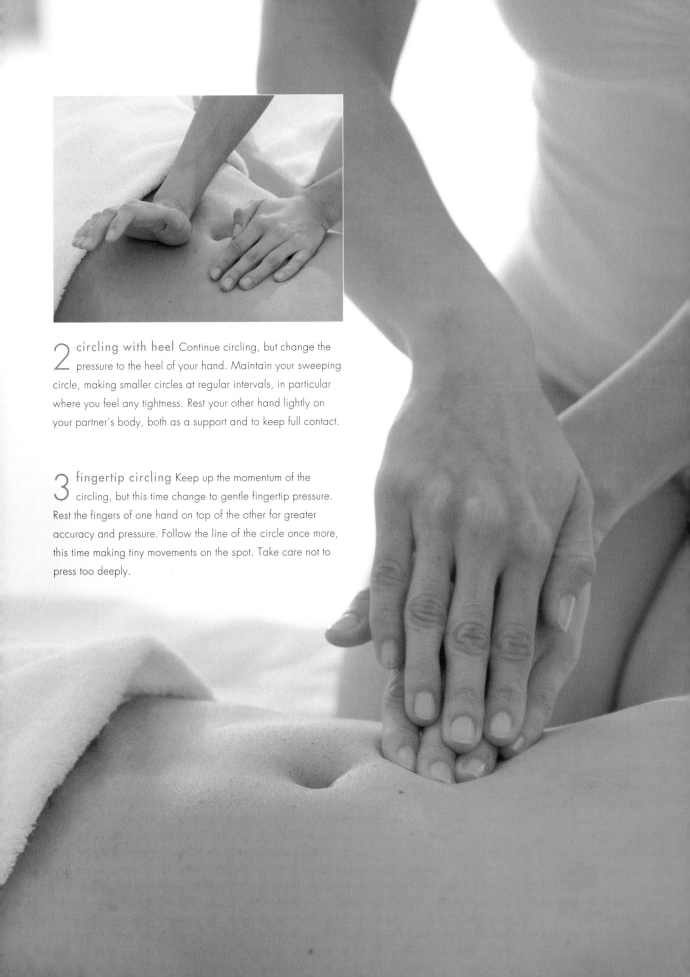

2 circling with heel Continue circling, but change the
pressure to the heel of your hand. Maintain your sweeping
circle, making smaller circles at regular intervals, in particular
where you feel any tightness. Rest your other hand lightly on
your partner's body, both as a support and to keep full contact.

3 fingertip circling Keep up the momentum of the
circling, but this time change to gentle fingertip pressure.
Rest the fingers of one hand on top of the other for greater
accuracy and pressure. Follow the line of the circle once more,
this time making tiny movements on the spot. Take care not to
press too deeply.

4 **kneading** Lean over your partner and begin kneading the soft muscles at the side of the body, working between the hip and the rib cage. Push the muscles away from you, then make small rolls back toward you again. Knead up and down several times, without massaging over the front of the abdomen itself. This feels good and the muscles here give a satisfying twist.

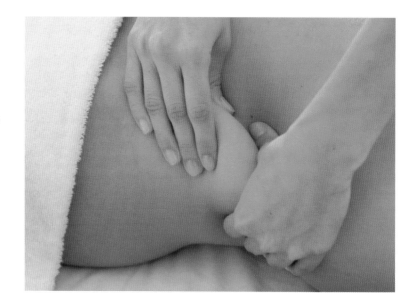

5 **pulling** Place one hand under your partner, just above the level of the hips. Pull your hand back toward you, at the same time starting the same movement with the other hand. Continue pulling for a few moments, then change position and perform these last two strokes on the other side.

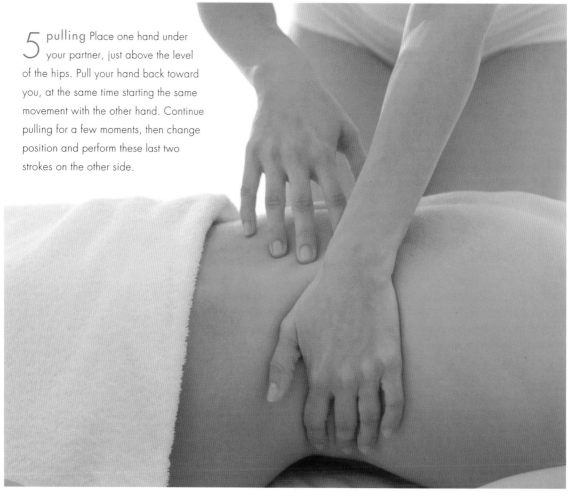

6 **resting** Place your palms softly over your
partner's abdomen and rest there for a moment,
allowing your hands to rise and fall with your partner's
breath. Feel the energy coming through the palms of
your hands toward your partner and think positively.
Then imperceptibly lift your hands away.

front of the legs and feet

This is the final stage of the further massage. If anything, you should slow your movements down, so that your partner has the sensation your strokes are lingering until the very last moment! In addition to the squeezing, kneading and wringing movements, you will be increasing pressure by using the heels of your hands and including work on the knees as well. Pay attention to the fronts of the thighs, where the muscles may require some work, but may at the same time be sensitive. The strokes on the feet are like the icing on the cake, releasing tension out through the toes. Your partner will find the final rocking to be a wonderfully freeing sensation and it closes the massage on a light-hearted note.

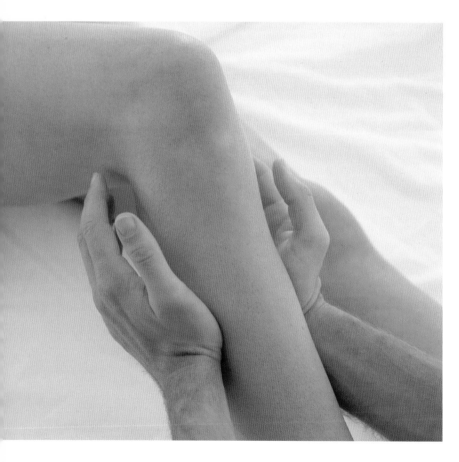

1 **squeezing the calf** Kneel at your partner's feet and effleurage over the leg. Then, begin squeezing up over the calf muscles as before. For extra pressure, use the heels of your hands to squeeze up the sides of the calf, rounding the movement off as you near the knee. Repeat the stroke up the length of the leg several times.

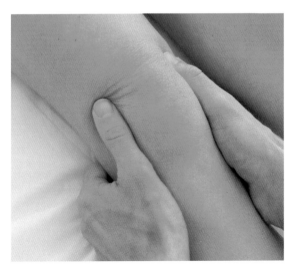

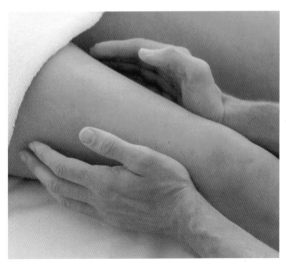

2 circling the knee Place both thumbs together at the base of your partner's kneecap. Now begin making very small circles, pressing in as close to the knee as you possibly can. Work your way up around the kneecap, with both thumbs circling at the same time. A firm, effective pressure will give a far-reaching release.

3 squeezing the thigh Moving further up your partner's body, continue squeezing up the thigh, again using the heels of your hands for extra pressure. Work in strips up the length of the muscles on the front of the thigh, rounding the movement off over the hip. Sense with your hands the areas that are needing attention.

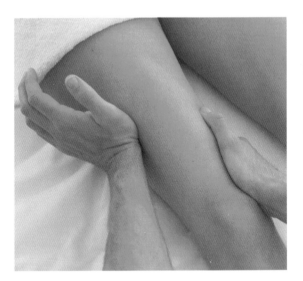

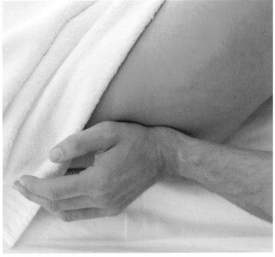

4 heel squeeze Lightly holding your partner's knee to support the leg (without applying pressure), use the heel of the other hand to squeeze up the side of the thigh, again rounding off over the hip. Do this stroke at least twice. Begin just above the knee and check the pressure, as this area can be quite painful.

5 circling the hip As you end the previous movement, place the heel of your hand at the top of your partner's thigh, in the curve just below the hip. Slowly circle away from you three times, pressing in with the heel so that the strokes penetrate more deeply. This movement is both soothing and releasing.

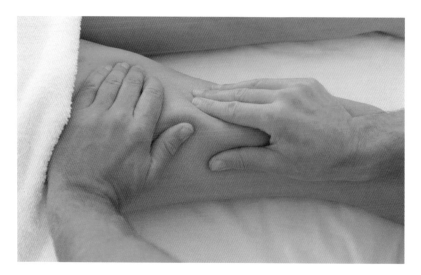

6 kneading the thigh Sit square-on to your partner. Begin to knead over the front of the thigh muscles, pushing into the muscles as much as feels comfortable, then making large rolls back toward you with your fingers. Work up and down the thigh, ending the strokes at the knee.

7 rocking under the knee This stroke comes in the middle of wringing. First, wring down the thigh. Then cup your hands loosely around the back of your partner's knee and gently rock from side to side, to loosen any tension. Keep the movements small, rolling the knee back and forth.

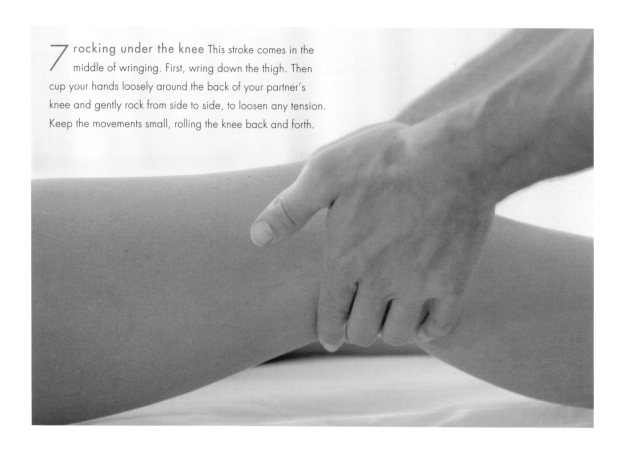

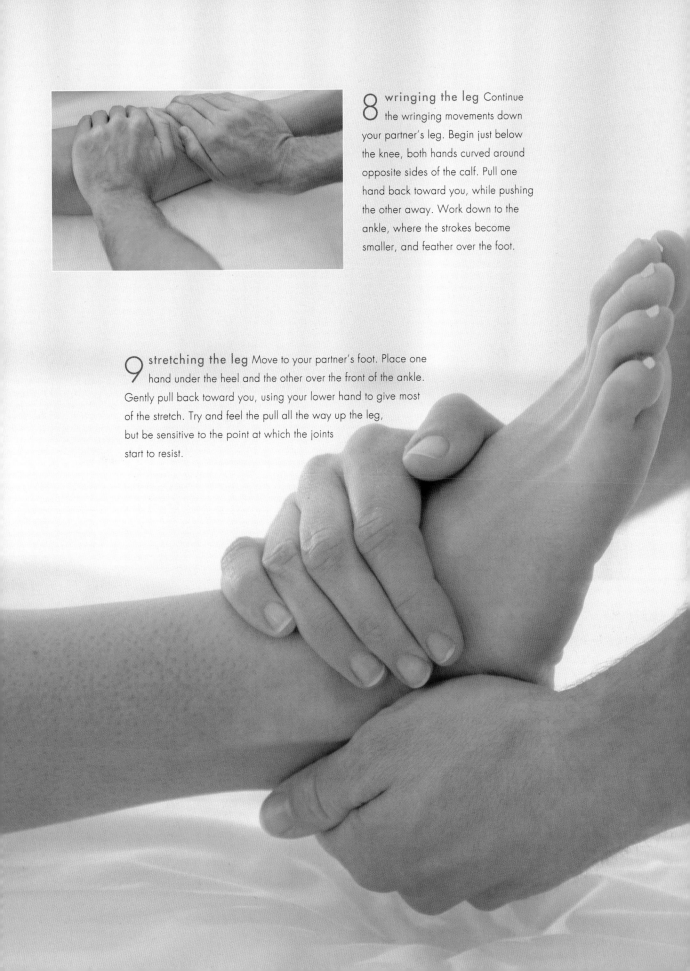

8 **wringing the leg** Continue the wringing movements down your partner's leg. Begin just below the knee, both hands curved around opposite sides of the calf. Pull one hand back toward you, while pushing the other away. Work down to the ankle, where the strokes become smaller, and feather over the foot.

9 **stretching the leg** Move to your partner's foot. Place one hand under the heel and the other over the front of the ankle. Gently pull back toward you, using your lower hand to give most of the stretch. Try and feel the pull all the way up the leg, but be sensitive to the point at which the joints start to resist.

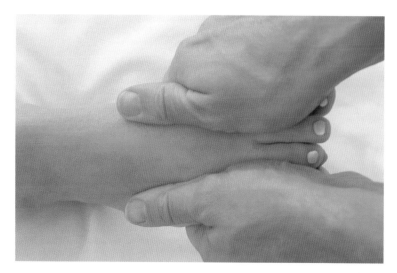

10 opening the foot Cup your hands around your partner's foot, fingers underneath, your thumbs flat across the top. Draw your thumbs apart, pressing over the top of the foot with the base of the thumbs. Draw toward the sides of the foot, then repeat the stroke. This is good for releasing tension and stretching the muscles.

11 pressing under the sole This complements the previous stroke. With your hands in the same position, press up under the sole of your partner's foot with your fingers. Use your thumbs to help arch the foot as you do so. Begin just below the ankle and work in a line down the centre of the foot toward the toes.

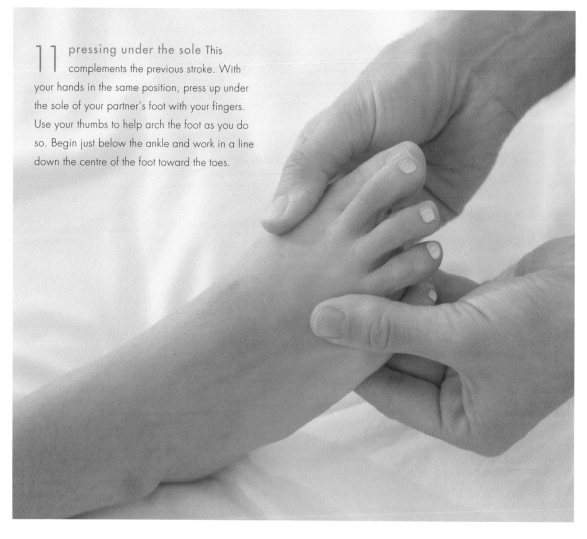

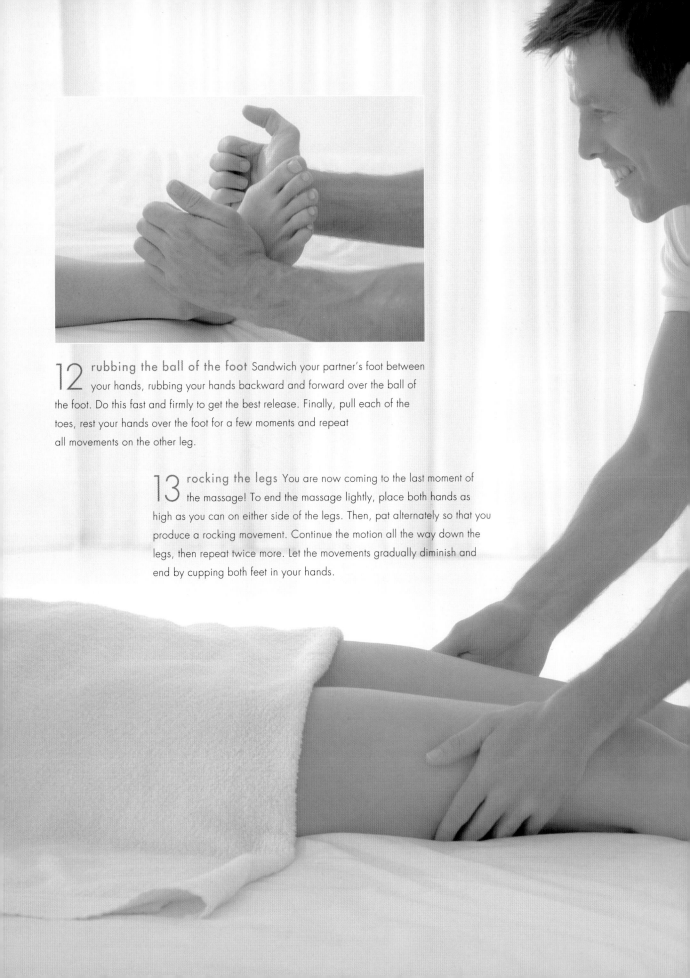

12 rubbing the ball of the foot Sandwich your partner's foot between your hands, rubbing your hands backward and forward over the ball of the foot. Do this fast and firmly to get the best release. Finally, pull each of the toes, rest your hands over the foot for a few moments and repeat all movements on the other leg.

13 rocking the legs You are now coming to the last moment of the massage! To end the massage lightly, place both hands as high as you can on either side of the legs. Then, pat alternately so that you produce a rocking movement. Continue the motion all the way down the legs, then repeat twice more. Let the movements gradually diminish and end by cupping both feet in your hands.

specific techniques

These techniques for specific purposes extend the ways in which massage can be used. Regard them as samples, for each section represents a whole different area of massage. Assuming a knowledge of general techniques, the strokes and points shown here will give you greater flexibility and a chance to adapt your massage to your partner's particular needs. In the case of sensual massage, a chance to let go with your sensuality! Experiment with the massage strokes, which you might now like to use more specifically to see what works best for you. These suggestions help to give an idea of the broad spectrum massage covers.

introduction to specific techniques

The sequence you have been following so far is a massage for general relaxation and tension release. However, massage can be used in a variety of different ways and on the following pages are some ideas for adapting your massage to specific circumstances and to the needs of you and your partner. Included are some techniques to deal with everyday ailments such as headaches, common areas of tension, as well as how to turn a massage between you and your partner into a sensuous occasion. And, if you are longing for a massage but find yourself without a partner just when you need one, you don't have to miss out. Simply adjust the techniques to yourself! These ideas are suggestions for you to try out and experiment with, which you may then decide to incorporate into longer massage sequences. The best idea is to get as much feedback as possible, then you will begin to get a clearer sense of what is successful for you and what is not. Be aware that everyone is different, so try the techniques on several people before making any judgements, and feel free to devise your own strokes if you find something that works particularly well. The more strokes that you have at your fingertips, literally, the more you will be able to help in different situations, and the more in demand you will be.

Common ailments

This first section is for common problems that can successfully be relieved through massage and helped by the use of essential oils. While professional training is obviously needed to tackle complaints of a serious or long-term nature, massaging or rubbing and pressing areas that are sore is an action that we all do instinctively. Using natural remedies, including

massage, is also a healthy, harmless and inexpensive way of dealing with minor aches and pains, with the added benefit of no side effects. When the body falls out of balance and diseases occur, it can provide its own solutions. In this respect, some knowledge of pressure points and their applications can be extremely useful. Before using these techniques, ask your partner to give you as much information as possible about the condition. See if you can establish between you the cause of the onset, any other conditions which may have exacerbated it or whether, if it is a recurring problem, there is a pattern related to it which can be avoided next time. You will often find that as you listen to people they will not only tell you what is wrong but also what they need to do about it or want you to do. Then use your knowledge and your intuition, and avoid pressure that is painful. *Remember not to actually diagnose or try to cure* – I am not recommending massage as a substitute for professional medical help – but you can be confident that the simple act of helping, plus the stimulation of your touch and attention, will be of real benefit.

Tension

While all massage aims at relieving tension, there are specific techniques that you can use to deal particularly with this problem. Again, the use of pressure points can be very helpful. As mentioned before, tension, especially in combination with environmental factors, is the cause of more problems than we might think and in one form or another, has become almost a part of everyday living. It can manifest itself as mental tension, where the mind simply will not switch off, and, or, physical tension, where the muscles are held protectively or defensively, which over a long time can result in a decrease in muscle range. Fibrotic tissue may also form in the muscles and fascia, which form the lumps or knots you can feel under the skin. People are often surprised that you can feel them, but it is actually quite easy. They also give you a clue as to where the work needs to be done. Tension, however, not only affects the site where you may feel it – the cause may lie in a totally different area – but affects the whole body, which becomes tight or closed, thus perpetuating the condition. Therefore, aim in your massage at loosening, relaxing and stretching, encouraging your partner to let go, even if just a little. To help your partner relax, use a light-hearted approach (rocking movements work well here) and encourage relaxation to come from within – it can never be forced from the outside. In addition, the use of soothing and relaxing essential oils can really work wonders.

Sensual massage

All massage is sensual to a certain extent. The skin contains millions of nerve endings relaying messages to the brain and each of these is extremely responsive. Every touch, whether light, deep or painful is registered. Massage naturally involves the senses, primarily touch, but includes the smell of the oils, the sound of the strokes (which should not be underestimated) and of course, a massage is visually sensual. It appeals both to the body and the senses. However, there is a world of difference between sensual enjoyment combined with a relaxing, soothing or therapeutic touch, and a sensual massage designed to arouse. A sensual massage is not something which should be sprung unannounced on your partner, but agreed upon beforehand. Then, it provides a wonderful opportunity to explore your sensuality, using touch to stimulate and energize the entire body. Through a combination of lingering massage strokes, gentle, inventive touches on sensitive areas of the body and your own knowledge of your partner, you can turn a massage into a sensual delight! Every part of you can

be brought alive. In fact, many therapists recommend massage to couples as a way of touching, arousing and getting to know each other without the pressure of sexual performance. Rather than focusing on sexual stimulation, bring attention to areas of the body your partner might not expect you to pay special attention to, and turn the whole body into an erogenous zone. Giving a truly sensual massage can be a beautiful, unselfish act of giving to someone you love. Once again, the use of essential oils will enhance the mood – several have the reputation of aphrodisiacs!

Self-massage

Self-massage is not a second best, but is, in fact, an excellent way of keeping muscles and joints relaxed and toned. In the absence of a partner, or to keep in shape between massages, it provides an easy and enjoyable way of helping yourself. You can always find the time to give your body a five-minute massage during the day and as often as you like. The advantages are that you know exactly the right pressures to use and can revitalize and lift your own energy, even when you feel tired. It is particularly good as a preventative measure as soon as you feel stress building up and has the added benefit of giving you immediate feedback. While the back is obviously the most difficult area to reach, with a little improvisation, you can cover almost the entire body, looking and feeling better in minutes. Massaging yourself fits in easily to any relaxation, exercise or beauty routine, and is a wonderful way to feel good about yourself, as well as providing invaluable massage practice. Set aside a time that is just for you and, as general rule, work from the top of the body down, ending with some general strokes where you are standing. Use stimulating strokes to wake yourself and keep your energy levels up during the day and relaxing ones, combined with some moments of deep, relaxed breathing at night, to dissolve the day's stresses and help you to sleep. Never for a moment imagine you too cannot benefit from the power of your touch.

headaches

A headache can range from a minor, dull ache to the full-blown pounding of a migraine. Instinctively we rub our painful head, but a massage from someone else is even better. Try out the following steps for general headache relief, always checking the pressure: on some occasions you can be so sensitive that only the lightest touch will do. First massage the neck, the cause of many headaches, moving the pain up and away from the head. Headaches may signal illness or infection, but are often due to digestive disorders, tension, eye strain, poor posture, sinus and menstrual problems, or reactions to food, drink or pollution. Try lavender, rosemary or a little peppermint oil, or simply relax in a lavender bath.

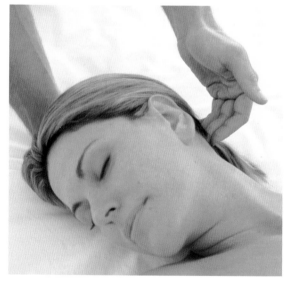

the neck Turn your partner's head to one side, supporting it on your hand. Then, ease your fingers along the top of the shoulder to the base of the neck. Keeping to the side of the spine, gently pull upward over the neck muscles to the base of the skull. Repeat several times, releasing tension with your fingers.

base of the skull Place your fingertips at the base of your partner's skull. Gently begin to rub the pads of your fingers in small circles, covering the base and back of the skull. Imagine any tightness releasing with your touch and your partner's pain literally dissolving. Repeat until you feel the tension releasing.

the eyebrows Place the tips of your thumbs to either side of your partner's nose, just below the inner part of the eyebrows. Now, slowly draw your thumbs up and outward, following the line of the brow to the temples. This will help to relieve congestion. Lift your thumbs gently away. Repeat the stroke several times, with the idea of drawing tension away from the eyes.

the forehead Place your thumbs together just above the eyebrows, in the centre of your partner's forehead. Press downward with the pads of your thumbs and gently draw outward to the temples. Repeat a number of these strips, each time beginning a little further toward the hairline. End by stroking very lightly.

arm relaxation

Many arm problems stem from tension in the back. Tight muscles restrict the movement of the joints, which causes an over-working of the muscles in the limbs and can lead to the nerves becoming irritated. However, with increasing problems occurring due to bad posture, prolonged computer use or desks at the wrong height, it is a good idea to make sure you keep the arms themselves as relaxed and trouble free as possible. The following movements help relax the muscles and joints. Adjust your office chair to the correct height, placing a block under your feet if necessary. Take frequent breaks, shake your arms out and alternate your actions between your right and left hand.

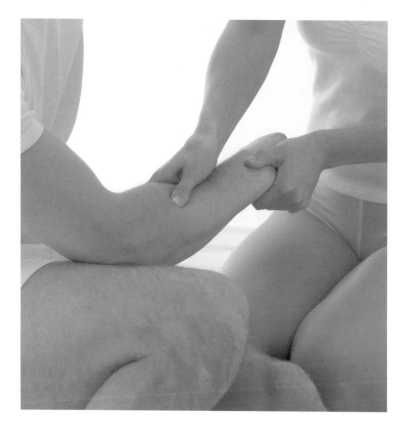

forearm press Support your partner's arm at the wrist. Place your thumb over the centre of the forearm, and press down between the bones. As you press, circle on the spot to increase the penetration of the stroke. Press down the centre of the arm at regular intervals to the wrist, keeping to the line of the bones.

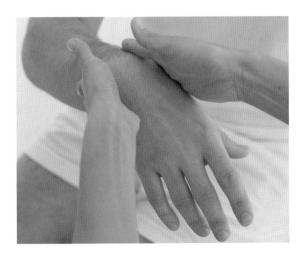

rocking the wrist Place your fingers lightly at either side of your partner's wrist. Roll the wrist from side to side between your middle fingers. The movement should be very quick. It will help to loosen the wrist and as long as your partner relaxes the hand, it will release to the fingertips at the same time.

squeezing between the bones Place your thumb over the top of the web between thumb and forefinger, with your fingers underneath. Draw down between the bones, squeezing between your first finger and thumb. Then repeat this movement between all the fingers across the hand.

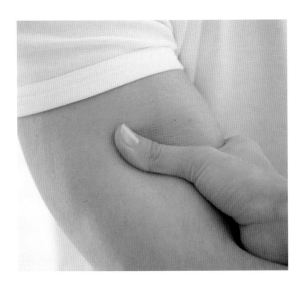

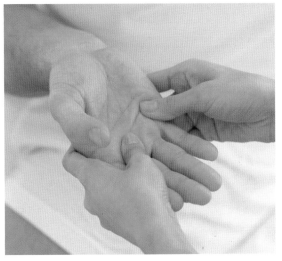

upper arm squeeze Support the arm at the wrist. Now, place your hand over your partner's upper arm muscles, thumb to one side, fingers to the other. Then press in, lift and squeeze and roll the muscles between your fingers and thumb. This feels wonderful. Continue working up and down the arm, releasing any tightness.

finger joint press Hold your partner's hand, palm upward, in your own. Use your thumbs to press in over the finger joints. You can press in quite deeply, working over, around and below the joints. Use both thumbs to massage each joint, pressing, rolling and circling between fingers and thumbs.

hip and lower back tension

Many people suffer from lower back tension, a complaint which often goes along with tightness in the hips. As the support for the rest of the spine, the lower back is extremely important, yet poor posture, strain through lifting, lack of exercise and badly supporting chairs all contribute to making this a weak spot. A tight lower back affects the rest of the spine. It may contribute to a lack of hip movement, which can then affect the legs, or cause sciatic pain. Here are some ideas for stretching the lower back, mobilizing the hip joint and loosening the surrounding fibrous tissue. Adequate back support, stretching and exercise can help to stop what may start off as stiffness from becoming more serious.

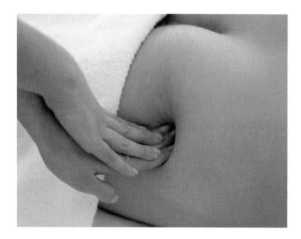

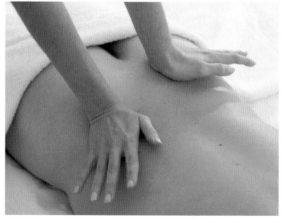

pressing the hip joint Sit to the side of your partner. Place the tips of your fingers behind the top of the thigh bone and slowly press inward. Increase the pressure very slowly as you penetrate the soft tissue, using your other hand to give support. Press and release around the joint. This movement will also affect the leg.

diagonal stretch Lean over your partner. Position both hands on opposite sides of the lower back, one level with the hip, the other slightly higher up. Now, give a diagonal stretch across the lower back. Lean in with your body weight and stretch the hands apart, without moving over the skin. Repeat the other way.

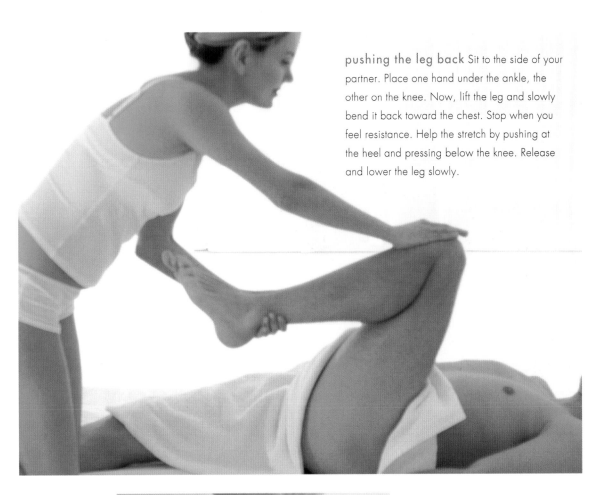

pushing the leg back Sit to the side of your partner. Place one hand under the ankle, the other on the knee. Now, lift the leg and slowly bend it back toward the chest. Stop when you feel resistance. Help the stretch by pushing at the heel and pressing below the knee. Release and lower the leg slowly.

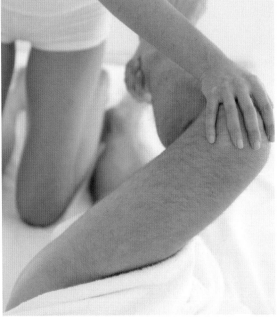

circling the hip joint Remain in the same position. Lift the leg and bend it toward the chest. This time, begin to circle the leg very slowly, supporting it under the foot and at the knee. Circle three times, making the circles as wide as possible, and stopping if your partner tenses. Repeat in the other direction, then gently lower the leg.

sinus problems

Sinus problems affect a number of people and can cause a great deal of discomfort and pain. The sinuses are mucus-secreting cavities that connect with the nasal passage through ducts. As a result of an infection such as a cold, the lining of the sinuses can become inflamed, leading to a production of excess mucus and blockage of the duct which drains the sinus to the nose. This creates a build-up of mucus, which leads to discomfort and headaches. If you have sinus problems, you may like to experiment with avoiding foods such as dairy products, sugar, wheat or potatoes, and concentrate on fresh fruit and vegetables. Eucalyptus, peppermint, basil and lavender oils are useful, especially if used as inhalations.

pressing inner corner of the eyes Although these points are usually associated with general headache relief, they can be very useful for sinus headaches. Place the tips of your fingers in the indentation beneath the eyebrows, in a line up from the inner corner of the eyes. Press in slowly, hold for two or three seconds, then release the pressure.

pressing under the eyes Place both thumbs just under the lower eye socket ridge and locate the depression in the bone, roughly half-way along. Press in slowly for three seconds, then release the pressure evenly. These points are particularly useful for easing sinus congestion.

pressing under the cheeks Place the tips of both fingers just under your partner's cheekbones, again locating the depression about one-third of the way along the bone, which you will find in a line down from the points under the eyes. Press in slowly with the tips of your fingers and hold there for three seconds, then release the pressure gently and evenly. These points will also help to relieve sinus congestion.

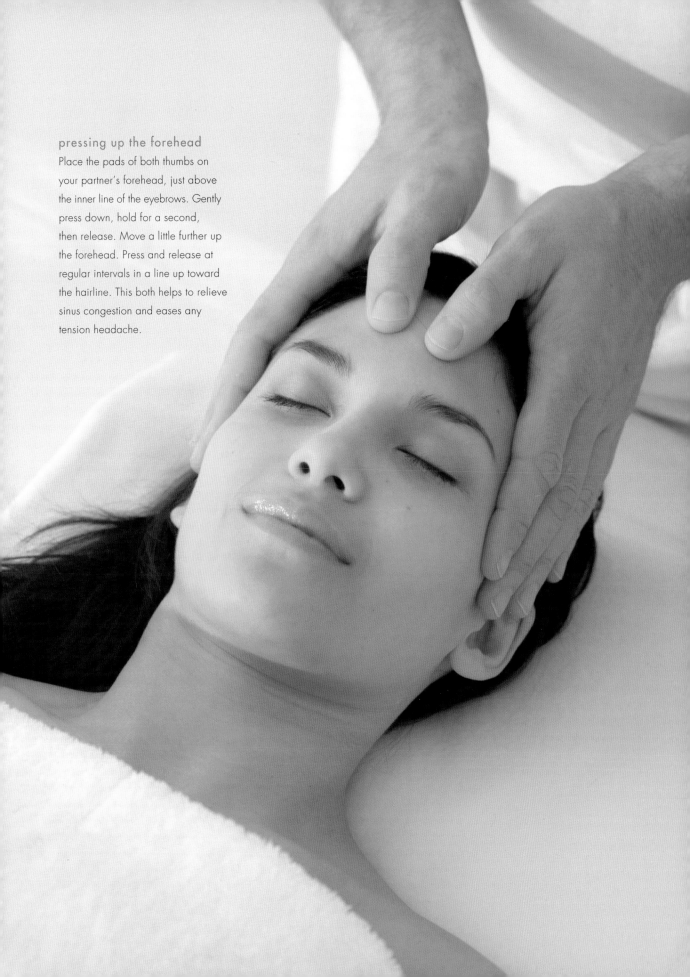

pressing up the forehead

Place the pads of both thumbs on
your partner's forehead, just above
the inner line of the eyebrows. Gently
press down, hold for a second,
then release. Move a little further up
the forehead. Press and release at
regular intervals in a line up toward
the hairline. This both helps to relieve
sinus congestion and eases any
tension headache.

the abdomen

Two conditions which can cause considerable discomfort and pain but which respond well to massage, are constipation and menstrual cramps. Cramps, occurring due to uterine contractions associated with heavy flow, can be eased by gentle massage and essential oils. Camomile, jasmine, juniper, peppermint, marjoram, cypress and melissa help if taken in a bath. You will notice that the massage strokes are not actually over the abdomen at all. Constipation is commonly due to tension, a diet of refined, starchy foods and not enough fibre. Again, relaxation, fresh fruit and vegetables, and reviewing problems and mental attitude may help. Black pepper, rose, fennel and marjoram oils can be useful.

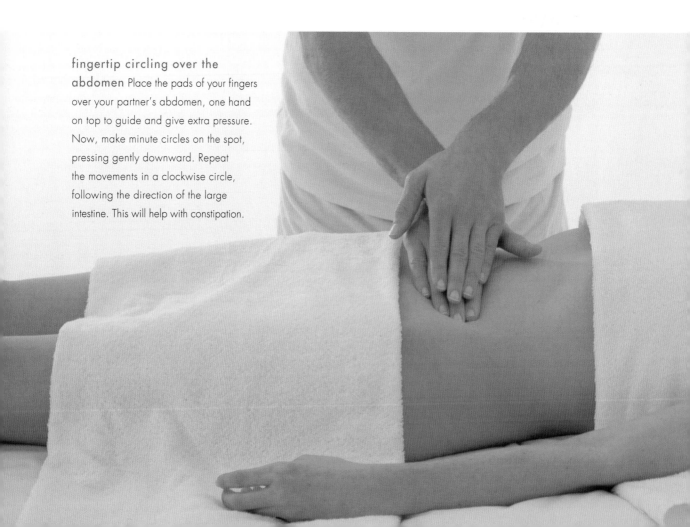

fingertip circling over the abdomen Place the pads of your fingers over your partner's abdomen, one hand on top to guide and give extra pressure. Now, make minute circles on the spot, pressing gently downward. Repeat the movements in a clockwise circle, following the direction of the large intestine. This will help with constipation.

circling the lower back When menstrual cramps are particularly bad, the last thing you want is to be touched. This stroke over the lower back, however, is warming and eases the pain. Place one or both hands over your partner's lower back. Slowly circle anticlockwise, making your circles large and comforting. Continue until the pain eases.

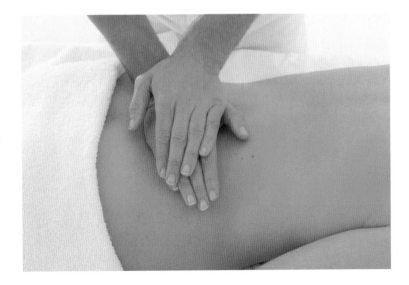

circling above the ankle This is for menstrual pain. Position your hand in a line three finger-widths up from the top of your partner's ankle. (The pressure point is located between the bones.) Now start to circle, pressing with the pads of your fingers. The movement should be slow and deep, and centred over the bones.

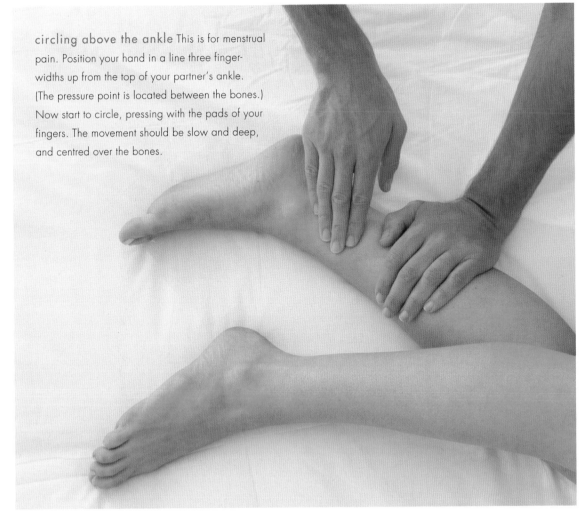

tension headaches

Headaches can sometimes be caused simply through tension. Stressful situations, pressures and confrontations, an information overload or overcrowded schedules can all cause persistent anxiety and the release of chemicals within the body. These can build up, resulting in headaches which are further aggravated by muscular tension brought about as we deal with these situations. However, why not try the following strokes instead of reaching for the aspirin? These movements will help with tension release and encourage the body to relax. Essential oils of rosemary, marjoram, melissa, rose or lavender can also be extremely useful where headaches are associated with nervous tension.

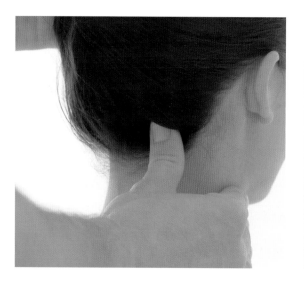

pressing under the skull Stand behind your partner with one hand on the body for support. Now, lightly place your thumb at the base of your partner's neck and follow the spine upward until you come to the hollow just below the base of the skull. Press gently but firmly for two seconds and then release. This has an immediately relaxing and uplifting effect. Only do this once.

kneading the neck Support your partner's head from underneath with one hand, then place the other hand at the base of the neck and gently knead your partner's neck muscles. Make sure your fingers stay to the side of the spine. Work up toward the skull and back again, gently lifting the muscles to encourage tension release. Then repeat on the other side.

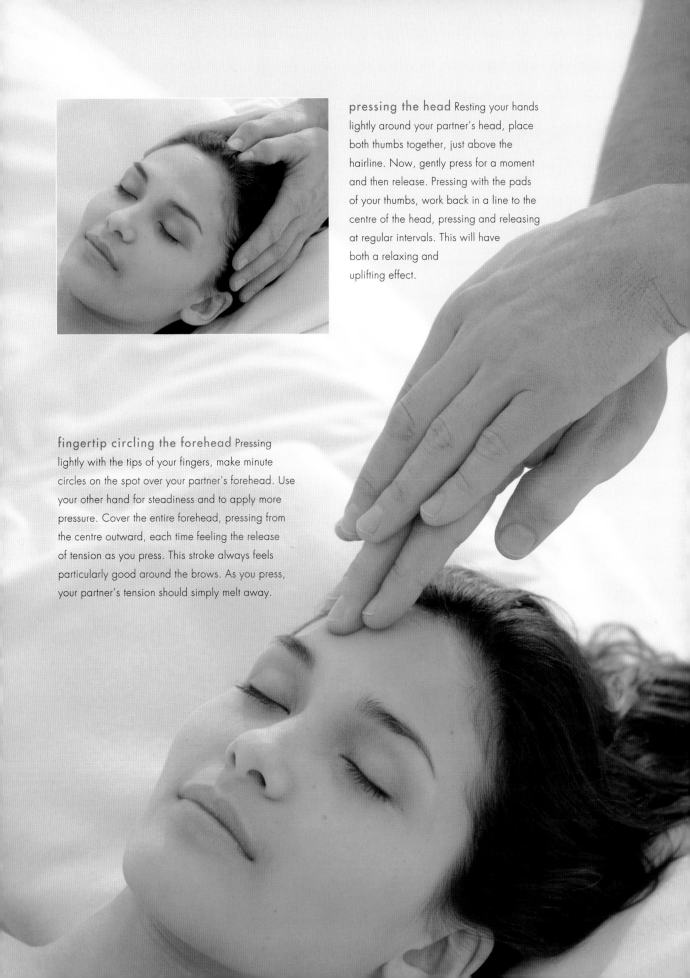

pressing the head Resting your hands lightly around your partner's head, place both thumbs together, just above the hairline. Now, gently press for a moment and then release. Pressing with the pads of your thumbs, work back in a line to the centre of the head, pressing and releasing at regular intervals. This will have both a relaxing and uplifting effect.

fingertip circling the forehead Pressing lightly with the tips of your fingers, make minute circles on the spot over your partner's forehead. Use your other hand for steadiness and to apply more pressure. Cover the entire forehead, pressing from the centre outward, each time feeling the release of tension as you press. This stroke always feels particularly good around the brows. As you press, your partner's tension should simply melt away.

facial tension

Surprisingly, the facial muscles can store a great amount of tension. When we feel tense, the body immediately becomes tight and closes up. A clenched jaw, gritted teeth and fixed smile all contribute to tight muscles, which are often not felt until released. To counteract these effects, it is important to relax the jaw, keep the tongue and mouth loose and the throat open. Relaxing the face can bring about an immediate change in mood and softens the appearance, which can become hard and pinched, giving a negative message. Try out these release techniques and remember that gently inhaling, then mentally breathing out tension as you exhale, is an excellent pick-me-up remedy.

jaw release Sit at your partner's head and reach forward to the chin. With your thumbs above and fingers below, ask your partner to relax the jaw, and then gently open it as far as possible. Make sure your partner does not help. Close the jaw, then repeat the movement several times to help your partner relax.

drawing a smile Place your thumbs over your partner's cheeks, just to either side of the nose. Then gently draw your thumbs over and around the cheeks, lifting the facial muscles into a smile. Ask your partner to help by softening the face. Relaxing and also giving a smile inside can have amazing results for your partner.

raking the hair This movement feels wonderful over the head and has a beautifully soothing effect on the face. Sitting behind your partner, rake your hands through the hair right over the head, keeping close in to the scalp. Work from the hairline to the back of the head, remembering to work back from the temples. This stimulates the scalp and feels uplifting.

lifting the head With your partner lying flat, place your hands under the base of the skull and then slowly raise the head as far as comfortable. Make sure your partner gives you all the weight and does not try to help. At the peak of the lift, ask your partner to relax and gently exhale, breathing out any tension.

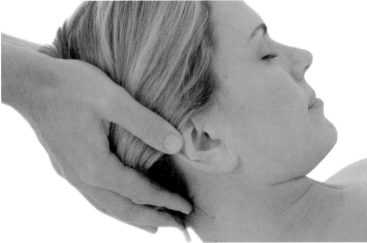

back tension

As anyone who has ever suffered from a bad back will know, the effects can be absolutely devastating. While problems by that stage need professional attention, many difficulties have their origin in muscular tension. Poor posture and tight muscles can seriously affect the movement of the joints, which results in compression and even further restriction of movement. Help maintain a relaxed back through regular massage, focusing on squeezing and pressing the muscles outward. Using pressure points will help. The key here is gentleness. Always move into a stroke slowly and only increase the pressure once you feel the back is relaxed. Otherwise your partner will respond by tightening further.

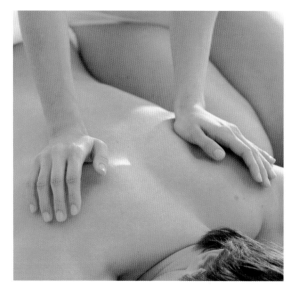

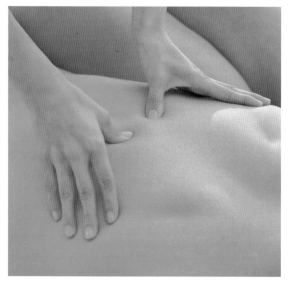

stretching between the shoulder blades Sit to your partner's side and leaning over, place both hands between the shoulder blades, at either side of the spine. Pressing with the heels of the hands, slowly push out toward the shoulders, stopping at the shoulder blades themselves. Repeat the movement for a great releasing stretch.

pressing between the ribs Place the pads of your thumbs over the muscles to either side of the spine, starting just above your partner's lower rib. Now, press into the muscles between the ribs and release. (Keep to the side of the spine.) Move up the spine, pressing and releasing after each rib, until you reach the base of the neck.

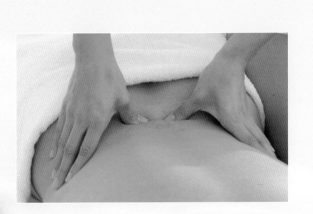

pressing the sacrum Place your fingers to either side
of the spine and locate the dimples at the top of the sacrum
(the bony triangle at the base of the spine), with your
thumbs. Now, move slightly inward, until you come to
a depression in the bone, press, then release. Move
down the spine and repeat three more times.

rocking Sit to one side
of your partner and lean across
to place your hands on the broad
bands of muscle running alongside the spine.
Press in with your heels, rocking gently away from you.
Your partner's whole body should respond to the movement.
Rock slowly up and down, focusing on loosening and releasing
tension from the muscles, and then repeat on the other side.

sensual massage

To make your massage sensual, simply approach the strokes in a different way. You can still use the familiar massage movements, but their quality and your intention will be different. Concentrate on the feel of your touch and the responses of your partner's body, using your hands sensitively to arouse and excite. Let your strokes linger. Use your fingertips to caress, explore and tantalize, building upon every sensation. Focus on the sensitive areas of your partner's body. Aphrodisiac oils include sandalwood, patchouli and ylang-ylang. Add to the intensity by inventing gentle touches of your own, using not only your hands but feet, breath, hair. Aim simply to delight and captivate your partner.

stroking with hair Use your body in creative ways in order to heighten your partner's senses. Brushing your partner's body with your hair feels wonderful. Trail your hair along your partner's back, over the soles of the feet or palms of the hands, gently flicking the ends of your hair over the skin. Always keep your attention focused on your partner's body. Discover and invent new ways of touching.

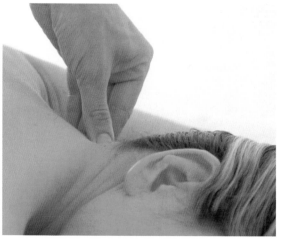

kneading over the neck muscles Use your thumb and forefinger to gently knead over the neck muscles, softly releasing any tension. This feels particularly good before and after turning the head. Squeeze and lift the muscles, continuing up through the hair and toward the base of the skull. The back of the neck is an extremely sensitive area. Every single attention to detail will make your partner feel special.

pulling the hair Gently finger and pull at your partner's hair, giving little tugs at the roots and stroking the strands right up to the very ends. This is a wonderful way of ending a massage over the head and neck. Everyone loves having their hair gently touched, caressed and played with.

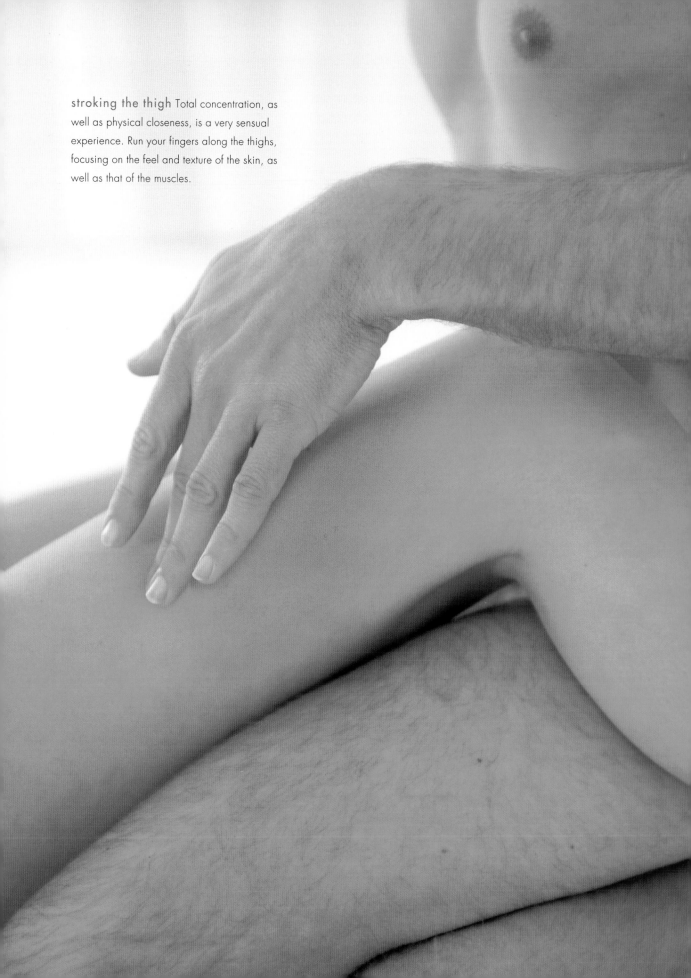

stroking the thigh Total concentration, as well as physical closeness, is a very sensual experience. Run your fingers along the thighs, focusing on the feel and texture of the skin, as well as that of the muscles.

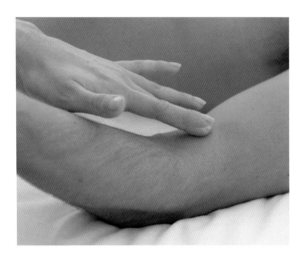

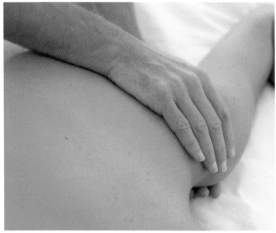

stroking the elbow crease Explore the sensitive parts of your partner's body. Stroke along the elbow crease, gently dragging your fingertips over the skin and making soft, slow circles around the joint. Then, brush lightly and allow your touch to trail away off the body. Every part of your partner's body can become a sensual focus.

pushing across the shoulder blade Gently support your partner's body from underneath, then use the heel of your hand to ease the muscles over the shoulder blade, pushing toward the joint. Work slowly and thoroughly, trailing your strokes down the arm. This is a warming and tender stroke. Releasing tense muscles is caring in action.

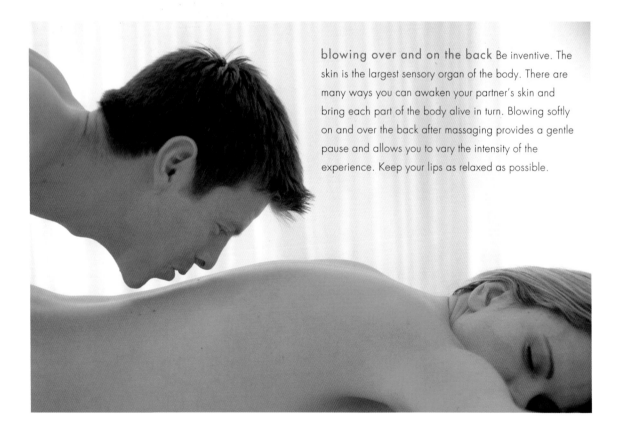

blowing over and on the back Be inventive. The skin is the largest sensory organ of the body. There are many ways you can awaken your partner's skin and bring each part of the body alive in turn. Blowing softly on and over the back after massaging provides a gentle pause and allows you to vary the intensity of the experience. Keep your lips as relaxed as possible.

stroking the shoulder Use your fingertips to gently trace over your partner's skin. Circle, draw, brush and caress with every finger and every part of your hand. Use your touch to stimulate the skin before massaging an area, to convey tenderness, to relax or comfort, soothe away tension or arouse. Experiment with the position of your own body so that while you are releasing tension, you are remaining physically close.

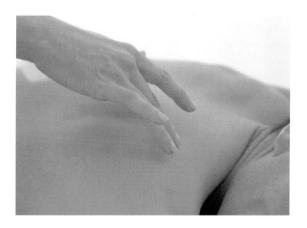

arm stretch Use creative touches to make your massage special. Raise your partner's arm and slowly pull the arm back behind the head. Grasp each other's wrists as you perform the stretch, so that your partner is playing a more active part. This gives the stretch a whole different feel.

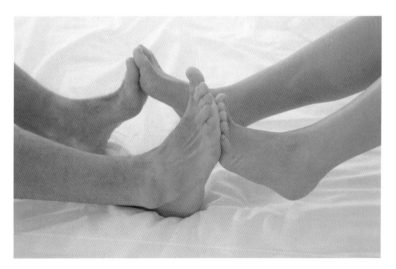

mutual foot massage A mutual massage is always a great idea. Try this one for the feet. Bring your feet together and pushing firmly against each other, use the toes, heels and balls of your feet to press over the soles of your partner's, covering as much skin as possible. Then rest, just toes touching.

caressing the hands In sensual massage, you can be creative with your bodies. Delicately run your fingers over your partner's hand, lingering over every detail. Touching softly, even when you are so familiar, opens up whole new ways of seeing your partner. It is an immensely powerful statement.

self-massage

The following pictures give some ideas that you can use for massage on yourself. If you are at home, a comfortable but firm surface such as an upright chair or the floor, with plenty of space to move, is ideal. Experiment with light and firm touches and feel how your body responds to both. Your responses can change depending on your mood. Be as inventive as you like, but be sensitive to vulnerable areas, especially the neck and lower back. You can massage using soothing or uplifting oils on your skin, but part of the appeal is that these movements can easily be done through the clothes. If time is a problem, the exercises are easily adapted to an office chair or desk, or, if you are really tired, to your bed!

shoulder kneading To release shoulder tension, place one hand over the top of the opposite shoulder. Knead and squeeze the shoulder muscles with your fingers and the heel of your hand. Work in toward the angle of the neck, and then out toward your arm.

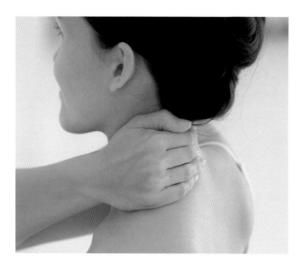

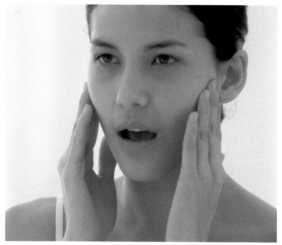

kneading the neck After kneading the shoulder, continue the movement more gently up the neck. Keeping your fingers to the back of your neck, squeeze gently between the heel of your hand and the balls of your fingers. Work up the neck to the skull and back several times, your fingers to the side of the spine.

circling the jaw To find the right place to circle, open and close your jaw, and place your fingertips where you feel the muscles working. With your jaw relaxed and open make large, slow circles over the muscles, using the tips and balls of your fingers. This movement is wonderful for releasing facial tension.

pulling across the forehead Place your hands so that the tips of your fingers meet together right in the centre of your forehead. Then, slowly draw your hands apart until your fingers reach your hairline. Keep the stroke really soft and as you draw your fingers across, feel all the tension dissolving.

abdomen circling Sitting in a relaxed position, place your hands flat against the centre of your abdomen, fingers pointing downward. Draw your hands slowly upward, separating them as you circle outward. Bring them together at the bottom of the circle, and draw them upward again. This is great for relaxing the abdomen.

kneading the side Place your hands at the side of your abdomen and grasp a roll of flesh with one hand. Begin a kneading movement by pushing away from you with your thumb and rolling your fingers back toward you. Knead up and down the side of your body, using alternate hands. This not only tones up the muscles, but helps relax the lower back.

pushing across the chest Placing your fingertips on your chest, just to the side of the breastbone, push the fingers firmly out toward the arm. Work in strips, from just under the collarbone to just above the breasts. This releases tightness in the upper chest.

circling the chest Use the balls of your fingers to make very small, firm circles across the top of your chest, using the same guidelines as before. It feels better if you keep the circling going outward and feels particularly good between the ribs.

heel circling the chest Although it looks a little awkward, this is an extremely effective way of working the pectoral muscles. Bring the heels of your hands to the sides of your chest, just beneath the level of the armpits. Press your heels firmly into the muscles and circle.

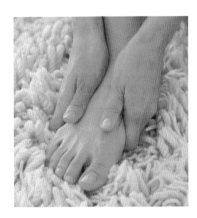

opening the foot Sitting so that you can comfortably reach your foot, place your fingertips together under the sole, the base of your thumbs together over the top. Slowly draw each thumb toward the side of the foot, applying slight pressure as you do so. This really gives the feeling of opening up the foot.

pressing the knee With your leg relaxed, use the balls of your thumbs to press right around the kneecap. You can press quite firmly, making tiny circles on the spot. This is really good for releasing any stiffness around the knee and the movements can also be felt in the calf and thigh.

rotating the ankle Making sure that the leg is being supported, place your hand firmly over the sole of your foot. Slowly rotate your ankle in both directions, making the circles as large as you can. This is great for loosening up the ankle joint and keeping it flexible, and will liven up the calf at the same time.

rocking the calf Place your hands either side of your calf, where the muscles are at their widest point. Rock your hands quickly and firmly from side to side, so that the muscles move with your hands. This is an excellent movement for loosening the calf, releasing tension and invigorating the entire lower leg.

pummelling the back A great way to liven up your back. Lean over and with your fists, pummel up and down your back as far as you can reach. This feels good on either side of the spine. Make sure your knees are bent and keep your wrists relaxed so the movements are sharp and fast.

lower back circle Lie on your back on a flat, firm surface. (This one does not work on anything that is soft.) Bring your knees to your chest and slowly circle your lower back against the floor. To ease the muscles in the lower back, make large and small circles in both directions, without lifting your hips off the floor.

pummelling the hips and thighs Lying on your side, support yourself with one arm and bring your upper leg forward with the knee bent. With your other fist, pummel up and down your thigh, hip and buttock, again keeping the movements short and lively. Then change sides. This really helps stimulate circulation.

pushing down the lower back
Rest your hands on your hips, thumbs facing the front. With your fingertips, feel for the dimples either side of the broad end of your sacrum (the bony triangle at the base of the spine) and push firmly downward along the line of the joint, without changing the position of your thumbs.

after massage

Just as time and thought needs to be given to prepare for a massage, so too you need to give careful attention to the way your massage ends to leave a lasting impression. Some knowledge of what to expect is particularly useful when you are just starting. You can then make sure both of you make the most of it. The after-effects of a massage should never be underestimated. For your partner, this means taking care to stay relaxed for at least half an hour after, and for you, it means making sure you replenish your energy and give some time to yourself. Plan for this time in your general massage preparation and be prepared for your friends to return for your services again and again!

the after-effects of massage

Everyone reacts differently after a massage. The response is very personal and has a lot to do with a person's mental or physical state beforehand. It is better not to go into a massage expecting a certain result, as this can be limiting and puts pressure on the person giving the massage. You can, however, expect that most people will feel much more relaxed. In addition, their bodies and personalities will be softer, their skin clearer, their colour healthier and their eyes clearer and brighter. Some people even have their most creative thoughts during a massage. Feelings may range from feeling mildly light-headed to something resembling euphoria. If your massage has been stimulating, then your partner may well feel more alert and energized.

Others feel an incredible sense of

heaviness and tiredness, and want to go off and sleep. Some people work up a healthy appetite, others feel as if they have just been exercising and may even feel a little sore. This is because massage takes the muscles beyond their present limit. Nearly everyone feels much looser physically and problems such as a tense neck or shoulders, sore backs and headaches will feel much improved, if they have not completely disappeared altogether.

It is possible your partner may feel emotional either during or after the massage, which may result in tears. This is perfectly normal. During a massage you are emotionally open and this may bring a release. However, it is simply part of the clearing process, and your partner will then feel much better. If your partner has little reaction, do not be disappointed or feel that your massage has not been effective. On many occasions, people have told me of amazing changes that have only taken place afterwards! As the person giving the massage, you too will be affected. Massage will make you feel more energized, more in love with life, it should make you glow!

guidelines
Here are a few helpful guidelines you might follow after the massage finishes:

• Leave your partner to rest for a short while. When ready to get up, advise them to roll onto their side. This is easier on the spine.

• After a massage, your partner should relax for at least an hour and drink lots of mineral water to cleanse the body. It is always nice to have some to offer.

• It takes from 30 minutes onward for essential oils to be absorbed and they may remain in the bloodstream for up to eight hours. To obtain the full benefits, your partner should avoid showering immediately afterwards so that the oils can take effect. When ready it is better to take a warm, not a hot, bath.

It is worth remembering that during the massage you will have been working for almost an hour, with your partner simply lying flat, and that your strokes will have been producing a state of relaxation. The change in blood pressure helps account for the sense of dizziness some people feel on getting up. There can also be a physical reaction where the symptoms might actually feel worse for a period of a few hours afterwards. This will gradually clear, leaving them feeling very good. Again, all of this is quite normal – massage is more powerful than you might think! Your partner will probably sleep soundly the night of the massage and the effects should last from two to three days after.

However your partner reacts, massage is an opportunity to make friends or bring you closer, and it is always nice to make an occasion of it. Setting aside an afternoon or an evening, not only for the massage, but for time to relax and talk afterwards, is always the best idea. You might then go for a walk, cook a meal or go out. Sharing the time together afterwards will turn your massage into a memorable experience.

feedback and reactions

Massage is a great time to get to know your partner better. Everyone reacts differently, has different needs and preferences, and each massage you do will be different from the rest. It is important to listen to your partner, to understand how they feel beforehand and how they feel and react afterwards. You will learn a great deal from the feedback, and the more you massage the more you will learn and the greater your confidence. Be as receptive as you can while you are massaging and encourage your partner at all times to tell you what feels good, what feels comfortable and if there is anything that does not feel good or that they do not like. Always check your pressure frequently at the beginning. If your strokes are too soft and gentle, they will feel ineffective; on the other hand, massage should never hurt. There is a certain sort of pressure that feels as if it is doing good, but there is another which simply feels like pain, and this you want to avoid!

While keeping within your own capabilities, be prepared to experiment and adjust the massage if necessary. If your partner simply wants to relax, be sure to set aside some time at the end to talk about how the massage felt and how their body reacted. You can learn a great deal from the feedback your partner gives you and any criticism should not be taken personally. It may simply reflect your partner's taste and be nothing to do with your technique. At the same time, your partner will probably want to know what you have noticed, such as areas of tension, if he or she felt relaxed and so on. Your partner will also be able to learn a great deal from you. Any reactions from either side are helpful and useful, even negative feedback, and will only lead to an improvement. The best way is to regard the massage as very much a joint effort so get involved, and above all have fun, enjoy your massage and relax!

adapting the massage

While keeping to your basic massage sequence, which is particularly important right at the beginning when you are just learning, it is important to be flexible and able to adapt the massage to your partner's needs. For example, if your partner is suffering from an injury, you would support the injury with a pillow and massage around but not over it. Similarly, if he or she cannot lie with the head to one side, place towels under the head or chest and have your partner lie with the hands supporting the forehead. Injuries, priorities, preference, sensitivity or lack of time may all mean that you need to adapt your massage to include certain areas of the body and simply brush lightly over other areas.

It may be that your partner is particularly sensitive. Shyness, uncertainty and vulnerability may all mean that you need to approach gently and to carefully choose your strokes. This is something you will gradually pick up on over time. Sometimes as you touch you will reap more reward by holding back just that little bit in order to go a little bit further. To touch more deeply and effectively requires a sense of timing, sensitivity and detachment not always easy to find. As the person giving the massage, you should look on your partner in a non-judgemental way, and if this is difficult for you, it is something you will need to develop. At all times, however, you should make sure your strokes are clear and non-intrusive, as your partner should never be made to feel uncomfortable. If your partner has to be active or work afterwards, then you will need to use the strokes in a slightly differently manner. Percussion movements and pressure points are particularly useful here, as they tend to have a more stimulating effect. Keep the general movements brisk and cup or hack over the back, for example, ending with light pummelling movements over the feet. Stretching and passive movements on the joints will also have the same effect, in preparing the body to be active. Bearing your partner's needs in mind through the massage will guide you, and your own alertness will have an effect on your partner's state of mind.

warming down

One of the wonderful aspects of massage is that it is as good to give a massage as it is to receive one! Giving massage revitalizes your own energy, totally transforming your mood, making you feel more positive, giving a sense of balance and providing enormous satisfaction. It is also great fun. In all the years I have been massaging, it never ceases to fascinate me. It is always different, often unpredictable and has never yet been boring! It is also a way of looking after yourself. You will notice a lot about your own body and needs. However, it is tremendously important not to underestimate the fact that massage involves huge amounts of giving, and it can be physically tiring, or emotionally draining. This is particularly true at the very beginning when you are concentrating on so many things at once and trying to get everything right!

It is important to make sure you receive a massage just as often as you give one. In addition, if you follow a few simple ground rules and stick to them, however good you get, you will be able to avoid the pitfalls that so many people fall into.

• Always set a time limit for the massage and keep a watch where you can see it. Be clear whether it is only you giving a massage or whether you are doing a swap with your partner, and if so, when that will happen.
• Always wash your hands at the beginning and end of each massage. This is not only for obvious hygiene reasons and to remove the oil, it also has a psychological effect.
• Never massage when you are particularly tired or bad-tempered, as this will often prove more draining.
• Set aside some time to give to yourself afterwards and allow a short period of rest. This can take whatever form you like, but the important thing is to take the time to recharge and put back what you have given out. Massage can be tiring and involves you with your partner in ways you may not be used to. At the beginning, especially, it is very easy to overstretch yourself. Relaxing, some simple stretching, a good cup of tea, a rest, some music, a warm, relaxing bath with lavender oil or salt are all ways of warming down afterwards, making sure you gather and replenish your energy.

conclusion

It is fairly easy to grasp the basics of the strokes and perform a massage that is pretty much technically correct. But how much more can be achieved when massage becomes an art, freeing up the tension formed from habitual body patterns and mental attitudes. Through massage you can tap into the spirit, creativity, spontaneity and naturalness which are so often buried under layers of routines, struggles and effort. Giving an inspired massage is like playing an instrument, as you watch the body respond, yield and soften, as tiredness and resistance give way to pleasure, harmony and balance. Massage is a transforming experience. It provides that sense of unity, connection and feeling of being whole. As you work on your partner, so your energy will increase, and as you join with the energy of your partner, so both of you will experience a degree of change. The fun starts when that added magical ingredient, which has nothing to do with the physical effects, takes over, and it is then that your strokes will become truly inspired!

index

A

abdomen
    further massage, 138–41
    problems, 160–1
    self-massage, 176
    simple massage, 80–1
acupressure, 98–9
adapting massage, 186
after-effects of massage, 184–7
ailments, 150
almond oil, 22
anatomy, 12–15
apricot kernel oil, 22
arms
    further massage, 128–31
    relaxation, 154–5
    simple massage, 74–7
    warming up, 29, 31
avocado oil, 22

B

back
    further massage, 104–13
    self-massage, 180, 181
    simple massage, 56–65
    tension in, 156–7, 166–7
base oils, 20, 22, 24
basil oil, 22
bergamot oil, 22
blood circulation, 15
blowing, sensual massage, 171
bones, anatomy, 14
breathing, warming up, 26

C

camomile oil, 22
carrier oils, 20, 22, 24

carrot oil, 22
chest
    further massage, 134–7
    self-massage, 177
    simple massage, 78–9
circling, 46–7
    thumb circling, 89
clary sage oil, 22
constipation, 160
contraindications, 17

E

effleurage, 36–7
emotions, 183
energy, stimulating, 32
essential oils, 20, 22–3, 25, 183

F

face
    further massage, 124–7
    self-massage, 175
    simple massage, 72–3
    sinus problems, 158–9
    tension in, 164–5
feathering, 48–9
feedback, after massage, 186
feet
    further massage, 118–19,
        145–7
    self-massage, 178
    simple massage, 84–5
fingers, warming up, 29, 30
first touch, 33
forearm see arms
fragrant, soothing oil, 25
frankincense oil, 22
friction, 90–1

further massage, 103–47
    abdomen, 138–41
    arms, 128–31
    back, 104–13
    chest, 134–7
    face, 124–7
    feet, 118–19, 145–7
    hands, 132
    legs, 114–17, 142–7
    neck, 120–3

G

geranium oil, 23
grapeseed oil, 22

H

hair, sensual massage, 166, 167
hands
    further massage, 132
    simple massage, 76–7
    warming up, 29, 30–3
head
    warming up, 27
    see also face
headaches, 152–3, 162–3
heel pressure, 92–3
hips
    self-massage, 180
    techniques, 100–1
    tension in, 156–7

I

illnesses, 17
injuries, 17

J

jasmine oil, 23

jaw
  self-massage, 175
  warming up, 27
joints
  anatomy, 15
  techniques, 100–1
jojoba oil, 22
juniper oil, 23

K
kneading, 38–9
knees, self-massage, 178

L
lavender oil, 23
legs
  further massage, 114–17,
    142–7
  kneading, 31
  self-massage, 178–9, 180
  simple massage, 66–9, 82–5
  warming up, 30, 31
luxury base oil, 24
lymph system, 15

M
marjoram oil, 23
menstrual cramps, 160, 161
muscles
  anatomy, 12–13
  tension in, 11, 150–1
  warming up, 28
mutual massage, 172

N
neck
  further massage, 120–3
  self-massage, 175
  simple massage, 70–1
  warming up, 27
neroli oil, 23
nervous system, 10, 15

O
oils, 20–5
opening, 45
organs, anatomy, 13

P
pain, 17
patchouli oil, 23
peach kernel oil, 22
percussion, 96–7
pregnancy, 17
preparation for massage, 16–17
pressing, 50
pressure points, 98–9, 150
pulling, 42–3

R
raking, 51
relaxation, 10, 26–33, 154–5
relaxing oil, 25
rich, soothing oil, 25
rocking, 94–5
rose oil, 23
rosemary oil, 23

S
safety, 17
sandalwood oil, 23
self-massage, 151, 174–81
sensual massage, 151, 168–73
shoulders
  self-massage, 174
  techniques, 101
simple massage, 55–85
  abdomen, 80–1
  arms, 74–7
  back, 56–65
  chest, 78–9
  face, 72–3
  legs, 66–9, 82–5
  neck, 70–1
sinus problems, 158–9

skeleton, anatomy, 14
soothing oil, 25
squeezing, 44
stimulating oil, 25
stress, 10
stretching
  massage stroke, 52–3
  warming up, 28
strokes, 35–53
sweet almond oil, 22

T
techniques, 35–53
tension, 11, 150–1
  in back, 166–7
  in face, 164–5
  in hips and lower back, 156–7
tension headaches, 162–3
thighs see legs
thumb circling, 89
thumb rolling, 88
touch, 10, 11

U
uplifting and refreshing oil, 25

V
varicose veins, 17
vegetables oils, 22

W
warming down, 187
warming, stimulating oil, 25
warming up, 26–33
wheatgerm oil, 22
wringing, 40–1
wrist, techniques, 101

Y
ylang-ylang oil, 23

acknowledgements

My thanks to all the team at Hamlyn. To Jane McIntosh,
Clare Churly, Tracy Killick, Darren Southern and Jane
Ellis for their invaluable creative input and enthusiasm.
Thanks to Russell Sadur for the wonderful photography
and Nina Duncan for so ably assisting, to Toko for the
effortless make-up, and to models Ryan Elliott,
Jacqueline Freeman, Jodie McMullen and Stuart Reed
for making it all look so inviting. And to Sian Facer for
the original commission.

Thanks go to Mike Stone and W. Llewellyn McKone
D.O., M.R.O., lecturer in osteopathic sports medicine,
for their invaluable advice and time spent going
through the text, and to Wanda Sellar for advice on the
use of oils. My thanks to my massage teachers, in
particular to Sara Thomas, also to Gill Levy, Steve Bird
and Barbara Simons. Finally, thank you to everyone at
the British T'ai Chi Ch'uan Association and at Amrita
Dzong for their continuing help and inspiration.

You can contact Susan Mumford at
www.susanmumford.co.uk or e-mail her at
susan@susanmumford.co.uk.

Executive Editor Jane McIntosh
Managing Editor Clare Churly
Editor Jane Ellis
Executive Art Editor Darren Southern
Designer Miranda Harvey
Picture Library Manager Jennifer Veall
Senior Production Controller Martin Croshaw